MEMOIR OF TIMOTHY GILBERT.

TREMONT TEMPLE.

Published by LEE & SHEPARD, Boston.

MEMOIR

OF

TIMOTHY GILBERT.

BY

JUSTIN D. FULTON.

"THE GRANDEST ABOLITIONIST IN BOSTON."

A Slave-hunter's Tribute.

BOSTON:
LEE AND SHEPARD.
1866.

SECOND EDITION.

STEREOTYPED AT THE
BOSTON STEREOTYPE FOUNDRY,
No. 4 Spring Lane.

Presswork by John Wilson and Son.

TO THE

CHURCH AND CONGREGATION

WORSHIPPING IN TREMONT TEMPLE,

This Volume

IS

RESPECTFULLY, GRATEFULLY, AND AFFECTIONATELY

DEDICATED,

BY THEIR PASTOR.

PREFACE.

THE life of TIMOTHY GILBERT, for half a century conspicuously identified with anti-slavery movements in the church and in the world, furnishes abundant testimony that the disciples of Christ have led the way in producing and carrying forward that great moral revolution which has disinthralled a continent. Redeemed bondmen will find in this life facts and incidents of permanent value, because it is to the courage and fidelity of such men, who leaped straight into the heart of the conflict, whose steel rang true upon the flint of the rebellion, and brought out the fire which melted their chains, that they are indebted for all that distinguishes the present from the past, and makes America, for the first time, "the home of the brave, and the land of the free," instead of the land of the free, and the home of the slave.

The relation sustained by the subject of this Memoir to the revivals that have characterized the present century, which, culminating in Boston, can be best studied from his stand-point, will invite the

Christian and the student to drink from this fresh fountain of inspiration and hope.

The work performed by Deacon Gilbert in building Tremont Temple, and in making it an attractive sanctuary where the masses may, from week to week, listen to the gospel of Christ, should give the story of such a life a welcome wherever an interest is felt in the establishment of a "Stranger's Sabbath Home," in the centre of a great city. That life will be found full of incentive to self-sacrifice and noble deeds. The subject of it lived and wrought for God, and his works do praise him.

The author would express his gratitude to G. W. Chipman, J. W. Converse, and Cyrus Carpenter, Esqs., who, from the first, have manifested the heartiest sympathy for the work to which Deacon Gilbert consecrated his life. Mr. Chipman supplied the excellent likeness of his life-long friend, Mr. Converse furnished the faithful picture of Tremont Temple, — Deacon Gilbert's fittest monument, — and Mr. Carpenter has, from the first, rendered valuable aid in securing the publication of this Memoir.

The author has been to the book what the scaffolding is to the building. He cheerfully steps aside, now that his work is done, that the reader may see the man.

CONTENTS.

MEMOIR

OF

TIMOTHY GILBERT.

CHAPTER I.

INTRODUCTION.

The story is told of Oliver Cromwell, that once upon a time, while sitting for his picture, the artist tried to conceal a scar upon his brow. The hero, noticing it, chided the painter, saying, "*Paint me as I am.*" The artist complied with the request, but so managed it that he placed Cromwell in a meditative position, sitting with his head resting upon his hand, and his forefinger concealing the scar. We shall let Timothy Gilbert sit upright. Not believing in perfect characters, nor in model lives, but rather in one perfect character, and in one model life, which closed its testimony on earth with the "It is finished" of Calvary, we shall try and present the subject of this Memoir as he lived at home, worked in the shop, toiled in the church, and battled for his faith in man and his faith in God in the midst of an opposing world and a sleeping church. His life deserves to be written, because it refutes the infidel utterance that there is something incompatible with a faith in Christ and a devotion to the highest interests of humanity. Horace Mann, Theodore Parker, and others like them, never tired of declaring that to help humanity men must break loose from creeds. Here is a man that clung to his faith in Christ, in the Bible, in the rule of faith and practice adopted by his denomination in Jerusalem, where Peter preached and James was bishop, and which has characterized them through all the intervening centuries, and now distinguishes them in all lands and climes, and yet he won from a slave-hunter the title of being the *Grandest Abolitionist in Boston.*

His identification with the great revivals of 1841, and with efforts calculated to secure the salvation of souls, links his name to the religious history of Boston. His efforts in behalf of the apprentices and mechanics deprived of a place of worship, and his watchfulness, that enabled him to seize the golden opportunity, when, because of the wonderful work of grace going on in Boston during the winter of 1841–2, the lessees of Tremont Theatre lost some ten thousand dollars, compelling the holders of the property to throw it upon the market, he purchased it, and by the aid of others, converted it into a free place of public worship, in which all the seats on the Sabbath are kept free to every person, without distinction, entitle him to the homage paid to public virtue and private worth.

On the first Sabbath of July, 1865, while the Union Temple Church were celebrating the Lord's Supper,

Deacon Timothy Gilbert, being absent for the first time, selected from Philippians, second chapter, from the fourteenth to the sixteenth verses inclusive, this message, which he asked his pastor to carry to them as a humble expression of his desire concerning them: "Do all without murmurings and disputings, that ye may be blameless and simple, children of God, unreproachable in the midst of a crooked and perverse generation, among whom ye shine as do the heavenly lights in the world, holding forth the word of life for a ground of glorying to me at the day of Christ that I did not run in vain or labor in vain."

The exhortation, "Do all without murmurings and disputings," expressed in words the principle that ruled his life. Little did I know of the trials that bent his frame and that ploughed deep furrows in his heart. He was a silent sufferer. To the scenes through which he had passed, and the labors he had performed, he seldom made reference. Now that he has gone, and that I have turned over the pages of his memoranda, I see that his desire to be simple, unreproachable in the midst of a crooked and perverse generation, and to shine as do the heavenly lights in the world, his anxiety to hold forth the word of life as a ground of glorying, rather than to talk of what he had purposed and achieved, made him the quiet and unpretentious man, who lived and wrought for God, and passed on to his reward.

A Christian's life is worthy of prayerful consideration and of profound study. It is a volume, the pages of whose imperishable record bear inscriptions wrought by the finger of God. It opens into the hidden mysteries of the world's great life. In it we behold the motive power that influenced, shaped, and controlled society. It opens into a home, and reveals to us God's model idea of a father, of a husband or friend. In it we see the thread of an almighty purpose entering the woof of events, and giving coloring and character to the distinguishing features of an epoch. It opens into a church, Christ's great workshop; it leads you into the prayer circle, to the sanctuary among the poor and among the influential, and becomes a finite cog fitting into the wheel of an infinite plan, and touching the machinery of society, which was set in motion for the glory of God and the good of man. Flowing into political circles, it resembles a clear mountain stream, cleansing and purifying all with which it comes in contact. It never can be thoroughly comprehended or understood. It is the incarnation of God's purpose among men. The opinions uttered, and the efforts made, help to establish justice, and to construct the healthy organisms of an age. It resembles a productive mine. There is little seen upon the surface; but when you reach the sphere of his labor, you become amazed at the extent of the area blessed by his love and cultured by his care.

If we enter the home of Timothy Gilbert, and behold him presiding over his table, giving a hospitable welcome to strangers, making ministers and missionaries, bondmen and freemen, feel that his house was Christ's house, and that he was acting as the steward of his Master; into the church, and behold him ever ready to bear his burden, and ever yielding to the yoke, but never forward, never ostentatious; into the political world, and see how modestly and firmly he bore himself, — we shall see that it was never his purpose to occupy a conspicuous position in the eye of men, yet that it was his grand aim to hold an honorable, though a humble place, in the eye of God.

He had no aspirations for office. When the Liberty Party was weak, he accepted nominations; when it became strong, he rejected proffers and posts of honor. He had no desire to be considered a leader even in commercial circles. He desired "to do justly, to love mercy, and to walk humbly with his God;" "to shine as do the heavenly lights in the world."

That made him what he was as a mechanic, as an employer, as a manufacturer, as an abolitionist, as a politician, as a deacon. That made him consecrate his time, talents, and property to the furtherance of the various interests committed to his care. That made him the champion of the oppressed, the friend of the poor, and the benefactor of the young. Write up such a life, and you embody in enduring shape a record which becomes the distinguishing feature of an epoch.

It may truly be said of him that he comprehended the era in which he lived. He had a logical mind, and could follow premises to their legitimate results. Hence he was never behind, but generally in advance of, his age.

He foresaw the result of the anti-slavery contest, and predicted it, and acted up to his convictions. When General Ulysses S. Grant permitted General Robert E. Lee to surrender the forces of the Confederacy in a manner that relieved him, and the soldiers he led, from the humiliation of a general, open, and formal laying down of the arms of rebellion, he foresaw trouble, and at once declared, "Those men will not believe they are conquered." When the air was full of the pæans of victory, his eye detected the dangers which followed in the wake of northern instead of southern conciliation. Not fully believing in the president concerning reconstruction, and wholly disagreeing with him in regard to negro suffrage, he prepared with great care a statement of the case as he viewed it, and sent it to the president, feeling that in this way alone could he discharge his duty. His rule being, "Whatsoever thy hand findeth to do, do it with thy might," he never postponed until to-morrow what should be done to-day, and as a result, achieved Titanic tasks, and accomplished important results. Desiring to be, not a leader, but a motive power and a propelling force, he worked through others, and delighted to hold up the hands of those who battled for the truth, and while glorying in results, shunned fame.

religion, he was a long time struggling with the corruptions of his own heart. His will was perverse and terribly unyielding. At last grace triumphed, and he became a little child at the feet of Jesus. No sooner did he obtain the liberty of the gospel than he had great peace and great love for the souls of others.

When converted he was surrounded by Congregationalists. The study of the New Testament made a Baptist of him. That was enough. Opposition was wasted on him. A Thus saith the Lord was better than a Thus saith a creed or a minister. There was no Baptist church nearer than three and a half miles, in Belchertown. That church became his home. On January 5, 1817, he was baptized by Rev. David Pease, in the river covered with drift ice, while around him gathered the church, singing, —

"Christians, if your hearts are warm,
Ice and snow will do no harm;"

after which he walked more than half a mile without a change of garments, and without inconvenience. On the last day of December, 1818, he came to Boston, and went to work, as an apprentice cabinet-maker, with Levi Ruggles, and after various changes, learned the piano-forte business of Mr. John Osborn, and in time formed a partnership with Mr. E. R. Currier. At the dissolution of the partnership, he became the head of the concern, and maintained the position, through many vicissitudes of fortune, up to the time of his death.

Boston, when he entered it a stranger, had but forty thousand inhabitants. There were three Baptist churches. Rev. James M. Winchell was pastor of the First, Rev. Thomas Baldwin of the Second, and Rev. Daniel Sharp of the Third.

Uniting with the last-named church, he carried into the Sabbath school and prayer meeting the idiosyncrasies that characterized him through life.

The influence of Dr. Sharp upon him was of a marked character. It was a primitive period in American history. The missionary enterprise had taken possession of the minds of Christians. The story of Carey's success, of Judson's conversion, the need of coöperation on the part of the American church, the formation of the Massachusetts Baptist Missionary Society, of the Northern Baptist Education Society, the establishment of colleges and churches, were facts which filled the mind and engaged the thought of that polished and courtly preacher, who delighted in the pulpit to dwell upon the Christian graces, and whose outward life was characterized by unsullied purity and a sublime devotion to every good work. Nathaniel Ripley Cobb, the Christian merchant, was a member of the church when he joined it. Cobb was a year his senior in birth and in baptism. He was born near Portland, Me., November 3, 1798, was baptized in May, 1818, and died May 22, 1834, when but thirty-six years of age, after having won a noble position in Boston.

On September 30, 1843, O. S. Fowler, the celebrated phrenologist, gave this description of Mr. Gilbert's character: "He is noted for goodness and desire for benefiting mankind. He would do it by making them good first, and by that means making them happy. The object of his life is to make men happy, and not one man in a thousand has a larger organ of benevolence. He is a stanch, stable man, that is a pillar in society — one to be depended upon. He pursues his uniform course with dignity, respects himself, and is respected. He has more thoughts and ideas than words to express them. Is fond of the beautiful. Is good at planning and setting others to work. Would be a deacon in a church and a director in a bank, and has great tact in contriving ways and means for accomplishing his objects. Is plain, but hospitable, and would be likely to have many visitors, and an extensive circle of friends. Gives advice, and good advice; is pleased with the approbation of friends; is strictly honest; dislikes to be in debt. I think he could hardly help being an abolitionist and a leader in reforms, Sabbath schools, and wherever he can do the most good. Will believe nothing without proof; must see the reason, the law, involved. Would have made a good clergyman. He stands by the right. Would speak the truth at the cannon's mouth. Conscientiousness is one of his principal organs." Those who knew him can recognize the correctness of the portraiture. He was as fearless and honest as he was brave.

CHAPTER III.

HIS MANNER OF LIFE.

HAPPY New Year greeted the ear of Timothy Gilbert, on January 1, 1819, the morning after his arrival in Boston.

He was a stranger. He loved his home, he idolized his mother, and he felt that sensation of loneliness which comes to the heart when the anchor is lifted and the sails are spread, and the boat in which our hopes are embarked pushes out upon the unexplored sea of the future, and the light of home no longer greets the view. He was poor, but brave. No young man ever began life under more straitened circumstances; none ever grasped the difficulties of the situation with a braver purpose. We find him early seeking employment. How he attempted and failed, tried again and succeeded, is remembered by his friends. He entered the shop of Levi Ruggles to learn the cabinet business. He has good strong hands, an eye to the main chance and single to the glory of God, an honest heart, and good health. In learning his trade he is animated by a purpose that takes in a wide and an ambitious range. He is an apprentice. He expects to be an employer; hence he studies principles as well as the cunning of handcraft. He dives into the secrets of success, into the questions of profit and loss. Having mastered the cabinet business, he turns to the piano trade, and strikes the thread of his destiny, which, followed, leads to fortune and fame. His heart is full of musical emotions and sweet harmonies, and his ear is attuned to melody. Here, in like manner, he studies all parts of the business, and is never content while anything remains to be learned. He is not a busybody. He is not meddlesome. He talks little, and thinks a great deal. He tries to increase in knowledge more and more, and so studies to be quiet, and to do his own business, and to work with his own hands, as the apostle commands, that he may walk honestly toward them who are without, and that he may lack nothing. The Bible is the rule of his faith and practice. In the church he has a place, and he is ever in it. In the Sabbath school he feels that he has duties to discharge, and he meets his trusts in a manly way. His seat in the sanctuary is always filled. His pastor comes to know him, and to lean upon him. Happy pastor, surrounded by men like Cobb, Gilbert, Farwell, and a host of others! — men of brain, of heart, and piety.

Naturally enough and without pushing, E. R. Currier wants a partner. He does not need money so much as he needs a man. He has heard of that quiet, thrifty mechanic. He seeks him out, or is sought out, and a partnership is formed, and young Gilbert, who on the 1st of January, 1819, came to Boston a stranger, is now a partner in business, and has use for all he has acquired, and a sphere in which he may use his inventive faculty to his satisfaction. In less than five years he marries a wife, secures a home, erects a family altar, and becomes the centre of an influence, which, like the ripple formed by the falling pebble, shall widen in its circumference until it writes its record on distant shores.

Settled in business, he was brought into contact with new circles of society and fresh currents of influence. He took positions. He brought all questions to the light of revealed truth, and judged them by the standards furnished by God himself. This made him set in opinion. It was a characteristic of his, when, after long reflection and prayer, he reached a conclusion to believe it to be the mind of God. It was this conviction that made him determined, and at times overbearing. Instances abound when it was clear he was mistaken in judgment. He was fallible, like others, and often, perhaps, mistook inclination for duty, and desire for conviction. He was not tolerant, nor patient, nor pliable. It is related by an individual who was then a youth, and is now a man of prominence, that he was sought out by Mr. Gilbert, and invited to obtain an education at his expense. He began his course, and was accomplishing the work, when, in consequence of his not being up to his benefactor in anti-slavery convictions, he was told of the disappointment his conduct had produced, and informed that, in accordance with a resolution to give money to such purposes and in such channels that it should tell upon the interests of the bondmen, he should be compelled to forego in part the amount allowed him. The proud-spirited youth resented the indignity, gave up his course and the ministry. In this Mr. Gilbert made a mistake. He saw it afterwards, and regretted it. Yet this characteristic was a blessing instead of a bane. He loved the truth, and delighted to follow its guidance. He erred in judgment at times, because he was a man. Truth pleased and charmed him. It begot principles within his nature, and those principles ruled him. Like trees planted in the earth, they absorbed the nutriment which came in their way. They grew. Hence, to influence him, truth must range itself behind these well-established principles. He knew that he could not do everything. He knew that he could accomplish some one thing. To this he bent his energies.

This made him take certain advanced positions. In looking about him, he saw that the churches were asleep in regard to the woes inflicted upon the race by slavery and intemperance. Believing that "Immanuel" — God with us — is with us to save us, he grasped the truth that "God is with us to save us by being God for us and God in us." On the one hand, *God for us by* taking the place of the sinner; and on the other hand, God in us by uniting himself to the sinner. The power of the gospel consists in this: that it not only reveals God's work for us when he took our place in the person of his Son, bore our punishment upon the cross, so that we might go free, but also God's work in us when he unites himself to us in the person of his Spirit, to renew and purify our hearts by the communication of his own love and righteousness. God for us! That convinces us of our sin; that takes away our fear. God in us! That assures us that the work once begun will be completed by the feeding of our inward life from his own divine fountains.

This, and not the force of an unconquerable will, made him strong, valiant, and invincible in his determination to aid forward the cause of Christ as the hope of the world. God was in him, he was in God.

This made him thoughtful and suggestive. It was a pleasure for him to live in sympathy with public men. His suggestions were not whims born in a moment, and to be swept aside by a breath. When he mentioned a subject and proposed a line of policy, it was the result of diligent and wise thinking. If his view made little or no impression when first mentioned, he would bide his time; but the sun was no more sure to rise than he was to bring the idea up in another shape; and even if it should be scouted and ignored, believing in it himself, he would consecrate himself to its furtherance and diffusion. This made him persistent and unyielding at times to an unpleasant degree, but it pushed him on in his beaten path, and made him the pioneer of important movements and reforms.

His manner of life as an employer and business man was characterized by idiosyncrasies peculiarly his own. He was kind, but exacting. He had ways of his own in transacting business, and disliked to be jostled by the ways of the world. He would have lived more pleasantly in London than in Boston, in England than in America. He depended for success not upon tinselry and show, but upon substance and merit. His pianos were well made, and, as was frequently stated, "in quality, strength of tone, finish, and durable manufacture, they are unsurpassed." He was especially fond of family music, and accordingly took sincere pleasure in introducing the "Æolian Attachment," combining the power of the organ with the sweetness of the piano. The Æolian Attachment, invented by Coleman, is a wind instrument of the softest and most delicate tones, and is so united to the piano-forte that the same key-board controls both instruments, so that either one of the two instruments may be used, or both together, blending in delightful and undistinguishable harmony. Of this instrument Mr. Gilbert was very fond; and indeed it is difficult to conceive of an instrument better adapted to accompany and assist the human voice, or to express the deepest emotions and sweetest experiences of the human heart. At the family altar the hymn books were passed around, and all sang. In singing he worshipped, as well as in reading and prayer. In selling instruments he would never disguise a fault or press a virtue. His pianos were great favorites in the South. They were easily kept in tune, and their music was soft and pleasant to the ear. He was known in his business to be an abolitionist, and would never compromise principle to secure favor. A North Carolinian, having purchased and paid for a piano, turned upon him, and said, "Mr. Gilbert, you are an abolitionist." "I am." "That money is the product of slavery." "Well," said the fearless soul, "I guess it won't help slavery while in my possession." "But are you not principled against receiving it?" "No; I hate slavery, not the money." "That is honest," said the tall Carolinian, and shaking hands, went his way, impressed by the bearing of the fearless deacon. His manner of life as a politician is known to but few. He had no aspirations for office. But he loved work, and was glad of influence.

Early in life he came to believe in human freedom. It resulted from his faith in Christ, the Saviour of mankind. The tie that bound him to God, linked him to the race. He regarded the cross of Christ as the standard of hope, and the gospel of Christ, preached and practised, as the power of God unto the salvation of men. The roar of that terrible tempest which came near levelling the superstructures of hope had been but faintly heard, when Timothy Gilbert, in the prime and flush of a young and vigorous manhood, consecrated himself to the cause of the down-trodden slave. Having made up his mind that slavery was the "sum of all villanies," that it was the violation of God's law written in Bibles and in the constitution of human nature, that the oppressed needed help to break the oppressors' yoke, he resolved to lend a helping hand.

The idea took deep root in his nature. It did not ruin him, as it ruined thousands. It did not make an infidel of him, and cause him to revile the church and revile the ministry. He did not deny the divinity of Christ, because he contended for the humanity of the negro. He followed Christ, and worked for man. He accepted the truth, and gave it liberty to influence his life. It did influence that life. At times it ruled him, and made him a terror to evil doers, and a praise to them who do well. Checked and held back by timid and conservative friends, it swelled within him like a mountain torrent. But he gave bounds to the throbbing emotion, and mastered the indignation that burned like a fire within, and walked firmly if quietly, sternly if peacefully.

Review a few facts. Believing that the negro should

be treated as a man, he invited one to take a seat beside him in his pew. It created talk. It made him odious. The pastor did not approve it, brethren did not like it. He persisted in two things. First, in his right to treat the negro as a man and a friend. Second, in his right to his own seat in the house of God. The excitement produced an unlooked-for result. It made him feel the importance of a free-seated house of worship. The seedling was planted.

In the course of time he joined the Federal Street church, having been assured that there would be no objections to his taking into his seat any whom he might desire. It may perhaps be stated as a fact, that had it not been for this discussion, and for his subsequent experience in obtaining seats for the young mechanics about him, the purpose to build Tremont Temple had never been formed.

He came to Boston in 1819. It was a wonderful year. Then began the anti-slavery agitation in Congress. It will be remembered that previous to the year 1819, the admissions to the Union had been of a slaveholding and non-slaveholding state alternately. As Alabama was to come in as a slave state, it was claimed that Missouri should come in as a non-slave state.

The slaveholders resisted, and claimed that the provision of the treaty ceding Louisiana territory to the Union carried with it the right to hold colored men as property.

State sovereignty lifted its hydra heads, and contended that Congress could not interfere with slaveholding without infringing state rights. The restrictionists refused to admit that to hold slaves was any right of the citizens of the United States. They went on to argue that as slavery was an enormous evil, totally contrary to the principles of the American government, for Congress to admit it, when it had the power of exclusion, would be at once a gross dereliction of principles, and a sacrifice of the interests of labor and laboring men to those of the comparatively small and much less meritorious class of slaveholders.

It is not difficult to imagine the effect of words like these upon the heart and mind of the young mechanic. His soul was stirred. He grasped the central truth, and clung to it for more than forty years, through evil as well as through good report.

The history of the rise and progress of abolition in the United States waits to be written. The principles that underlie the movement are as old as God, and run parallel with the progress of the race. Wherever the gospel has exerted its influence, slavery has been felt to be a sin. In our revolutionary struggle, the claims of human nature were asserted. General Gates, the hero of Saratoga, emancipated his slaves in 1780. In the papers preserved by Mr. Gilbert are records of emancipation movements and abolition meetings, beginning with the year 1783, when, in Woodbridge, Middlesex County, N. J., on the 4th of July, the first anniversary of our independence after the revolutionary war, an abolition meeting was held, at which time a Dr. Bloomfield emancipated fourteen slaves. The scene must have been impressive. Great preparations had been made, and an immense concourse of people had assembled. A platform was erected just above the heads of the spectators, and at a given signal the doctor, followed by his slaves, seven on the right and seven on the left hand, mounted the platform and addressed the multitude on the subject of slavery and its evils, and in conclusion said, "As a nation we are free and independent: all men are born equal, and why should these, my fellow-citizens, my equals, be held in bondage? From this day they are emancipated; and I here declare them free and absolved from all servitude to me or my posterity." Then calling up one advanced in years, he said, "Hector, whenever you become too old or infirm to support yourself, you are entitled to your maintenance from me or my property. How long do you suppose it will be before you will require maintenance? Hector held up his left hand, and with his right drew a line across the middle joints of his fingers, saying, "Never, never, massa, so long as any of these fingers remain below the joints." Then turning to the audience, the doctor remarked, "There, fellow-citizens, you see that liberty is as dear to the man of color as to you or me." The air now rang with shouts of applause, and thus the scene ended. Such incidents charmed him. He felt that they were types of great possibilities. He was proud to recall to the recollection of men who were fond of calling abolitionists fanatics, that Abolition Societies were formed as early as 1774, and that John Jay, Alexander Hamilton, Benjamin Franklin, and Benjamin Rush occupied prominent positions in them. He recognized Washington as an abolitionist, and took pleasure in recounting the triumphs of the party of freedom. Yet even here his glorying was linked to the cause of Christ. He acknowledged with pleasure the obligations of the country to Benjamin Lundy, born in Sussex County, N. J., who consecrated himself to the service of the negro, and labored to establish Abolition Societies as early as 1815, and who, after incredible hardships and privations, came to Boston, and had the honor of awakening a passion for the cause of freedom in the breast of William Lloyd Garrison, who, born in Newburyport, Mass., in 1805, was then, at the age of twenty-three, editor of the National Philanthropist, an organ of the temperance movement. It was, however, his boast that while Mr. Garrison learned the value of human freedom, the worth of a human soul, though enshrined in a dark setting, he and William Crane, of Baltimore, and Clarkson and Wilberforce, learned the same glorious truth from the spirit inculcated by the gospel of Christ.

The supposition widely prevails that freedom has been obtained for the enslaved in spite of the church. It is a groundless supposition. The church has led the way. Christians in this nineteenth century have made the age in which they live glorious, because of what God has wrought through them and by them. The history of the triumphs of this principle is not half written, when the exploits of the so-called Liberty party are chronicled. Much is said against the church, and little is said against any one outside of the church; just as much is said against Christians, and little is said against infidels, not because Christians or the church are worse than infidels or worldlings, but because so much more is expected of those who profess a love for and an allegiance to Christ.

On the hill-top of this century, as of others, posterity will behold the face of some prominent Christian, who, through evil report and good report, has battled for the rights of man and the glory of God. If the church, as a body, has been slow to take hold of reformatory measures, it will be seen that the tardiness has not been in consequence of a want of a love for man, but from an apprehension that such a course of procedure would distract attention and imperil the interests of souls. In the great convocations of the Baptists, Presbyterians, and Methodist churches, it is not true that those who resisted slavery agitations loved slavery or believed in it. They felt that the church and the societies to which they belonged were under obligations to render unto God the things which belonged to God. If this made them slow to render unto Cæsar the things which belonged to Cæsar, it is pleasant to discover that the fear arose, not because of a love for Cæsar, but for Christ.

The lives of Timothy Gilbert, Nathaniel Colver, William Crane, Jacob Knapp, Elon Galusha, and a host of others, prove that the interests of bondmen found advocates in the church as fearless, as uncompromising, as valiant as ever were found in the ranks of reformers. We do not wish to disparage the efforts made by Liberals and so-called infidels. They have wrought well if not wisely; but we do contend that a comparison made in the church with the efforts made outside of it, will serve to reflect lasting honor upon the church as an agency of good even in promoting the temporal and political advancement of mankind.

Space will not permit extended sketches of contemporaries; but a reference to them is essential to this record of a life which identified itself with the beneficent and heroic in the church and in the world. It is well to remember that seven years before Timothy Gilbert came to Boston, William Crane, born in Newark, N. J., 1790, went to Richmond, Va., where, in 1815, the same year that Lundy formed an Abolition Society, he with others founded the African Missionary Society, with a view solely to missions in Africa. In the same year he established a night school, where, for three nights in the week, colored people were taught to read and write. Lott Cary, the pioneer missionary to Africa, received a large part of his education here, and was fitted for his responsible work in the land of his fathers and among the neglected people of his own race.

The influence of Isaac T. Hopper's life in Philadelphia and New York had much to do in giving shape and character to the spirit of reform. Born in New Jersey in 1771, he joined the Society of Friends, early removed to Philadelphia, and became prominent as the friend of the slave. It is a little singular that New Jersey, which in politics has ever been on the pro-slavery side, should have furnished a birthplace to so many advocates of freedom. The story of Mr. Hopper's life has been written by L. Maria Child. The incidents of that life in detached portions have for more than a half a century occupied their share of public attention. We can remember the effect of those accredited tales, and can easily imagine the influence they exerted upon the heart and mind of the youthful mechanic, alive to the interests of the cause of freedom. A slave comes by night to his unpretending home, and he relates the story of his escape, of his being discovered in the City of Brotherly Love, and of what Friend Hopper did for him. As a specimen, take this treasured record of "Mary Halliday," a very light mulatto girl, in the service of a Mr. Francis, a slave of a Mrs. Sears, of Maryland.

She was discovered. Mrs. Sears claimed her. Mr. Francis, valuing her services, asks Mr. Hopper to try and purchase her for three hundred and fifty dollars. Mrs. Sears refuses to sell, and declares her purpose to take her back to Maryland, and to make an example of her.

"I hope thou wilt find thyself disappointed," replies Friend Hopper. Finding himself beaten there, and disappointed in the result, he resolved to carry the case to a higher court. For that purpose he obtained a writ "*de homine replegiando*," and when the suitable occasion arrived he accompanied Mary Halliday to the mayor's office with a deputy sheriff to serve the writ. When the trial came on he urged the insufficiency of proof brought by the claimant. The mayor replied in a peremptory tone, "I have already decided that matter. I shall deliver the slave to her mistress." Friend Hopper gave the sheriff the signal to serve the writ. He was a novice in the business, but, laying his hand upon her shoulder, said, "By virtue of this writ I replevin this woman and deliver her to Mr. Hopper." Her protector immediately bade Mary go home with him. Her mistress, seizing her arm, said, "She shall not go." The mayor was confounded and perplexed, and inquired what the writ was. "It is a '*homine replegiando*,' replied Friend Hopper.

"I don't understand what that means." "It is none the less powerful on that account. It has taken the woman out of thy power, and delivered her to another tribunal." The mayor was puzzled, but told Mrs. Sears to let her go. She inquired, "What am I to do?" He replied, "Ask Mr. Hopper. His laws are above mine. I thought I knew something about the business, but it seems I don't." And so Mary in the end got free.

A slave accompanies his master — longs for freedom — is told to keep quiet six months — does so — wins his freedom after a frightful contest with his master. These stories filled the air.

There was something exciting in the hunt. Who has not seen the victim, with the fresh brand on arm and cheek, creep into the room, be fed and housed, and passed on? They came singly, and in companies of two, three, and four, to the house of Timothy Gilbert. These stories excited attention. This spirit of receiving slaves became infectious. Slaveholders came North after their chattels. Slaves crept South after wives and children.

Uncle Tom's Cabin was born of this spirit, that was formed by these years of smouldering fires.

Debates in neighborhoods and churches grew apace and waxed furious.

The Christian heart of Timothy Gilbert was ready for the work. His mind was made up. He was quiet, unostentatious, determined, full of shifts and subterfuges; believed God, blessed him for his care of the poor, and worked like a hero in the cause.

Look at the Congressional Debates, and we perceive in the discussion of 1819 the seedlings of the Kansas-Nebraska bill, and the anti-slavery agitation which shook the continent.

Cobb, of Georgia, fixing his eye upon Tallmadge, the original mover of the restriction in the Missouri compromise debate, exclaimed, that " a fire had been kindled which all the waters of the ocean could not put out, and which only seas of blood could extinguish" — a prophecy which Timothy Gilbert saw fulfilled.

Tallmadge replied, " Language of this sort has no effect upon me. My purpose is fixed. It is interwoven with my existence. Its durability is limited with my life. It is a great and glorious cause, — setting bounds to slavery the most cruel and debasing the world has ever witnessed. It is the cause of the freedom of man. If a dissolution of the Union must take place, let it be so. If civil war, which gentlemen so much threaten, must come, I can only say, let it come. . . . If blood is necessary to extinguish any fire which I have assisted to kindle, while I regret the necessity, I shall not hesitate to contribute my own. Are we to be told of the dissolution of the Union, of civil war, and seas of blood? And yet with such awful threatenings do gentlemen in the same breath insist on the extension of this evil and scourge — an evil brought on with dire calamities to us as individuals and to the nation, threatening in its progress to overthrow, along with the liberties of the country, all our notions of religion and morals. You behold southern gentlemen contributing to teach the doctrines of Christianity in every part of the globe. Turn over the page, and you behold them legislating to secure the ignorance and stupidity of their own slaves. The man who teaches a negro to read is liable to a criminal prosecution. The dark, benighted beings of all creation profit by our liberality, save those on our own plantations. Where is the missionary of hardihood enough to venture to teach the slaves of Georgia? Here is the stain, the stigma, which fastens on the character of our country, and which, in the appropriate language of the gentleman from Georgia, not all the waters of the ocean, only seas of blood, can wash out."

Timothy Gilbert was then twenty-two years of age. The church had a conscience at this time. Christians South, as well as Christians North, were awake to such appeals. We behold that handsome, black-eyed, thoughtful mechanic pondering these truths. He takes his stand. A principle is begotten within him. A negro is a man, and shall be considered a man. We shall see the results of this stand. Two years are gone.

The church shakes itself, and feels its fetters. Parties have formed and are forming. The opinion is entertained that slavery is a local sin, bound by state lines, and that freedom of thought and utterance shall not overleap them.

A few radical men in Boston believed that truth was of God, and scorned boundaries. In 1831 there came from Virginia a protest concerning an incendiary print being freely distributed among their people. Harrison Gray Otis, a former mayor of Boston, writes a letter, in which he says, —

"The first information, received by me, of a disposition to agitate this subject in our state, was from the governors of Virginia and Georgia, severally remonstrating against an incendiary newspaper published in Boston, and, as they alleged, thrown broadcast among their plantations, inciting to insurrection and its horrid results. It appeared, on inquiry, that no member of the city government of Boston had ever heard of the publication. Some time afterwards it was reported to me by the city officers, that they had ferreted out the paper and its editor; that his office was an obscure hole, his only visible auxiliary a negro boy, and his supporters a very few insignificant persons of all colors. This information . . . I communicated to the above-named governors, with an assurance of my belief that the new fanaticism had not made, nor was likely to make, proselytes among the respectable classes of our people."

Such was the state of things in 1831. Anti-slavery, said the Hon. Harrison Gray Otis, had an "obscure hole" for its headquarters.

Ah, it had more than that. The heart of God was its headquarters, and the hearts of his children, among whom proudly stood Timothy Gilbert, were the channel through which its currents found their way to this world.

It is well to notice how and why this subject has been kept before the people. At the outset champions found a home in every state of the Union. Brave words and glowing tributes fell from the lips of a Pinkney of South Carolina, a Randolph of Virginia, characterized by as earnest an utterance as ever distinguished an Adams or a Sumner. The war of 1812 began to draw the lines. New England opposed the South. In 1820 the battle became general. In 1831 John Quincy Adams stood forth in the House of Representatives as the champion for the right of petition. In 1837 the House adopted a rule, which was sustained by the Senate, ordaining that no petition relating to slavery, nearly or remotely, should be read, debated, or considered. The state authorities approved. Slavery was supported by the courts no less than by the fixed habits of thought and action among the people.

In 1832 the Nat Turner insurrection occurred in Virginia. It was well planned, but its author failed, and was destroyed. Henceforth colored preachers are banished from the pulpit.

In 1831 John Quincy Adams took his seat in Congress, two years after he retired from the Presidency of the United States. He is sixty-four years of age, but the fires of youth burn unquenched in his veins. In 1835 his congressional career attracted national attention. With all the ardor and zeal of youth, he placed himself in the front ranks of the battle which ensued on the right of petition, plunged into the very midst of the *mêlée*, and with a dauntless courage, that won the plaudits of the world, held aloft the banner of freedom in the halls of Congress when other hearts quailed and fell back. In these contests a spirit blazed out, as he led the "forlorn hope," which electrified the nation with admiration.

His first act was in relation to slavery. He presented, on the 12th of December, 1831, fifteen petitions, numerously signed, for the abolition of slavery in the District of Columbia. On he marched, when the most sanguine believed his almost superhuman labors would be in vain. Not so. Like the gnarled oak beaten by tempests, the sage of Quincy grew each day more hardy and more bold, as, unmoved by the storm raging around him, he battled for the right. His course was righteous. The air was full of a spirit that worked for him. Timothy Gilbert, in Boston, wrote petition after petition, which were signed and forwarded. Whoever came to his office had the privilege of hearing some fresh utterance. In the church, on the street, in his home, and in his place of business, he fanned the flame of liberty. The opposition in Congress, in abolishing the freedom of speech and the right of petition, to save an obnoxious institution, went a step too far. They made an attempt to place their feet upon the neck of a free people. There were too many men like Timothy Gilbert in the North. From one end of the land to the other there was revolt, upheaval, shame, confusion, and disaster. Abolition Societies were formed. Documents were circulated, while each day Adams followed petition with petition, now from the radical North and now from the slaveholding South, now from freemen and now from slaves, now that slavery may be abolished and now that it may be strengthened, until his enemies were confounded by his tactics, overwhelmed with confusion by his gathering reputation and increasing power, and scathed by his words of irony, denunciation, and sublime utterances in behalf of freedom.

He claimed that the South was bound and cemented together by a common intense interest of property to the amount of $1,200,000,000 in human beings; that this vast sum is invested in property which comes under a classification once denominated by a governor in Virginia as "property acquired by crime"; "which, in the purification of human virtue, and the progress of the Christian religion, has become, and is daily becoming, more and more odious; that Washington and Jefferson, themselves slaveholders, living and dying, bore testimony against it; that it was the *remorse* of John Randolph dying; that it is renounced and abjured by the Supreme Pontiff of the Roman Church; abolished with execration by the Mohammedan despot of Tunis; shaken to its foundations by the imperial autocrat of all the Russias, and the absolute monarch of Austria, — all, all bearing reluctant and extorted testimony to the self-evident truth, that, by the laws of nature and of nature's God, man cannot be the property of man."

"Recollect that the first cry of human feeling against this unhallowed outrage upon human rights came from ourselves; that it passed from us to England, from England to France, and spread over the whole civilized world; that after struggling for nearly a century against the most sordid interests and most furious passions of man, it made its way at length into the Parliament, and ascended the throne of the British Isles. The slave-trade was made piracy first by the Congress of the United States, and then by the Parliament of Great Britain. But the curse fastened, by the progress of Christian charity and of human rights, upon the African slave-trade, could not rest there. If the African slave-trade was piracy, the coasting American slave-trade was piracy; nor could its aggravated turpitude be denied. In the sight of the same God who abhors the iniquity of the African slave-trade, neither the American slave-trade nor slavery itself can be held guiltless." Such is a specimen of his style, and of fiery bolts he hurled against the tottering citadel of slavery. Soon he gained upon his adversary. Congressional district after district sent champions to his side. States reconsidered and resolved in his behalf. Church after church, and association after association, followed in the march to freedom, and kept step to the bugle notes of liberty. Soon he gained upon his adversaries. He saw the tide was turning, and then struck one masterly blow, not alone for freedom of petition and debate, but of bold and retaliatory warfare. Like the enraged moose of our western wilds, when the hounds are wearied, and when his blood is up, he pounced upon his assailants with crushing force, and offered the following amendment to the Constitution, to be submitted to the people of the several states for their adoption: "From and after the 4th day of July, 1842, there shall be, throughout the United States, *no hereditary slavery;* but on and after that day, every child born within the United States shall be free." In 1845 the obnoxious rule of the House was rescinded. The freedom of debate and of petition was restored, and the unrestrained and irrepressible discussions of slavery by the press and political parties began.

In the mean time the church had not been idle. In

Timothy Gilbert's parlor, anti-slavery meetings were of frequent occurrence. In his church his views were known. In the community he was a recognized power for the slave. In 1850 the fugitive slave law passed. We cannot describe the scenes in Congress, in Boston, and throughout the Union. Timothy Gilbert, on Wednesday, September 25, 1850, through the "Evening Traveller," addressed his fellow-citizens in these words: —

"This infamous bill has finally passed both Houses of Congress. My opinions may have but little weight with those who voted for it, but may help sustain the sinking spirit of some poor, disconsolate one, who, having fled from the land of oppressors, is anxiously looking to see if there is any one who will give him a cheering look or a kind reception, or who dares to give him a crust of bread or a cup of water, and help him on the way. Allow me to say to such a one, that if pursued by the merciless slaveholder, and every other door in Boston is shut against him, there is a door that will be open at No. 2 Beach Street [now No. 8], and that the fear of fines and imprisonments will be ineffectual when the pursuer shall demand his victim. If he enters before the fleeing captive is safe, it will be at his peril.

"I am opposed to war, and all the spirit of war, — even to all preparations for what is called self-defence in times of peace, — yet I should resist the pursuer, and not allow him to enter my dwelling until he was able to tread me under his feet. I will not trample upon any law, either of my own state or of the nation, that does not conflict with my conscientious duty to my God; but Jesus has commanded, saying, 'All things whatsoever ye would that men should do to you, do ye even so to them.'"

Pause a moment. The man is true to humanity — as true as was Theodore Parker, or Garrison, or Phillips, the thunders of whose eloquence shook Faneuil Hall, and resounded through the land. He did not turn away from Christ, nor ignore the divinity of the Son of God, while he battled for the humanity of the negro. He carried his love for Christ through all those years of obloquy and reproach; and boldly writes in a public paper his reason for his conduct, saying, "Jesus has commanded," and then proceeds with the argument. Placing himself in the condition of the slave, he says, "If, for no crime, I had been taken and sold, and deprived of all the rights of my manhood, and degraded to the rank of a beast of burden, not only deprived of the opportunity to labor for the support of my wife and children, but even deprived of their kind sympathy and companionship whenever the interest or will of my oppressors should require it, and I should, at the peril of my life, flee from my oppressors, and they should pursue me to the dwelling of some poor disciple of Jesus, — it may be that of a colored man, — and I should beg of him to protect me, and help me to escape from the pursuers' grasp, should I not hope, if he was a Christian, he would give me bread and water, and help me on my way, regardless of the fines and imprisonments that such a kind act might render him liable to? Could I expect to meet the approbation of my Lord if I did not do as much for the fleeing slave? Can there be a Christian in the land of the Pilgrims who will not do it, and besides do all in his power to prevent any one of those senators or representatives in Congress, who voted for that infamous bill, from ever again misrepresenting any portion of the friends of freedom in Boston or elsewhere? It is said, 'This is a law of the land, and must be obeyed.' To such I would say, 'Whether it be right in the sight of God to hearken unto you more than unto God, judge ye.'

"I prefer to obey God, if in so doing I must break the laws of men and be punished, rather than violate the laws of God, and obey the laws of men to escape fines and imprisonments, or even death." Signed T. Gilbert, Boston, September 3, 1850.

To this, as was usual in his letters, is attached a postscript. A friend once said, "Timothy Gilbert wrote letters for his postscripts. Read them, and you know why he wrote." In this postscript he explains why he calls the law infamous, and gives his reason in these words: "Because by it the man or woman who is charged with being a slave is deprived of all the means of self-defence allowed to those charged with crimes, and to be delivered up summarily, without the right of trial by jury, or any other proper means of proving the charge groundless. Is it a worse crime to be a slave than to be a thief or a murderer?"

Two facts deserve mention. That night, as soon as Theodore Parker had devoured the letter, while his heart was hot, he grasped his hat, ran round the corner, found No. 2 Beach Street, rung the bell, and said, "'Is Timothy Gilbert in?' Timothy Gilbert stepped into the hall, and then and there for the first time locked hands with that fiery apostle of freedom."

Last spring, in Virginia, I pictured the scene, and related this story, to three thousand negroes in Richmond. Their sighs and sobs revealed the fact that an answering chord of sympathy had been struck, while their conduct to our brothers all through the war, their kindness to the poor, escaped prisoners, to the wounded and dying, show that the effect of our kindness to fleeing fugitives has made a deep impression upon the loyal African heart.

There was another fact revealed to us by a scrap of history brought to our notice by the waves of war. We find the following in the "Massachusetts Weekly Spy," Worcester, October 29, 1862: —

"REBEL DOCUMENTS. — One of our correspondents with the sixth regiment has been kind enough to send us several rebel documents found in a lawyer's office in Suffolk, Va. The office has been taken for a guard-house, its owner, Nathaniel Reddick, being now in Jeff Davis's army. Among the papers is a receipt for 'one negro woman named Reuben,' signed by Reddick aforesaid; also a challenge to mortal combat from one Graham to a Dr. Bradford, dated 1796. The challenge appears to have been accepted, for, says the bearer in his return, 'His answer was, at the Cool Springs he would meet you at daylight on Sunday morning.' Whether or not either of the parties was killed is a matter of painful uncertainty. Last, but not least, we have a letter under date of New York, January 21, 1851, written by one of the Reddicks, and addressed to Benjamin, the lawyer, in which the writer gives a chapter of his experience in pursuit of a fugitive slave. The 'case,' we presume, will be readily recalled by parties in Boston. Riley, referred to in the letter, doubtless means Patrick Riley, who, if we mistake not, was a deputy under United States Marshal Devens. The 'man Gilbert' clearly refers to Timothy Gilbert, a well-known citizen of Boston, the manufacturer of Gilbert's piano-fortes. 'The factory' which the writer refers to can be none other that his extensive warehouse. The narrative is too interesting to keep, and notwithstanding the writer's request to 'keep things as dark as possible,' we give the letter entire: —

"NEW YORK, January 21, 1850.

"DEAR SIR: This morning very unexpectedly finds us in New York. We left Boston yesterday about three o'clock P. M., and arrived here last night about twelve M. Monday morning, about three o'clock, in disguise and in company with the officers, we went and guarded every street leading to the factory, and were perfectly certain of arresting the boy; thought there could not be a doubt, but were disappointed. We were then satisfied that he had got the wind of us. On Saturday evening, after I had written to you, one or two of the officers went in an adjoining house to the factory, and endeavored to see inside of the factory, and there discovered a boy answering fully the description of Lewis. On Monday morning, after we had failed in our endeavor to arrest him, having retired to our place of rendezvous, one of the officers stepped in with that morning's paper (the 'Commonwealth,' the main abolition paper of the city), and there the matter was blown. They had discovered these men around the factory on Saturday evening, and ferreted out their design, and the fugitives were immediately put on the alert; and also two *kidnappers and slave-stealers* were said to be in the city, and it gave them h—ll. We then had a consultation with Spencer, the marshal (Riley), and other officers employed, and they advised us to leave the city immediately, to allay suspicion. The marshal said he was positively satisfied, by our adopting that course, that he could soon succeed in arresting him. He, and all concerned, appeared to be much mortified that the thing should have got out, and he swears to have him at all risks. So we left the papers with such directions as were necessary, and are now in New York, and intend waiting a few days to hear from Boston. All of the officers are satisfied that they will know the boy, upon sight, beyond a doubt — one of them certainly saw him while we were in Boston.

"We have kept all of our proceedings a profound secret, and it is very necessary that secrecy should be preserved for some time yet. We are fully satisfied — or at least I am — that the boy is yet in Boston, and in the house of this man Gilbert, the owner of the factory. He is quite wealthy (the piano-forte man), *and the grandest abolitionist in Boston.* He will pay fugitive slaves more for work than any other persons, and give them the privileges of his private residence, table, &c.; has private watchers employed for the better security of fugitives, &c., &c.

"Keep things as dark as possible.

"Yours truly,

"F. C. Reddick."

We are glad to add, as a supplement to this letter, that the United States Marshal Devens has proven himself to be the friend of the slave. Mrs. L. Maria Child, in a recent letter, gives him the credit for offering to pay the eighteen hundred dollars required to free Thomas Sims, while, as an officer in the war, he has been not only a defender of the country, but the champion of freedom, and is now a firm and consistent advocate for negro suffrage.

Those words of the slave-hunter furnish a beautiful inscription for Mr. Gilbert's monument, and a fitting close to this portion of his career in behalf of freedom. "He was the grandest abolitionist in Boston." Grandest because his loyalty to man never shook or disturbed his loyalty to God.

In Scotland they tell of the grandeur of Ben Nevis, because the granite pushes its way up through the mica schist, while the porphyry crowds up through the granite, and crowns the summit. That mountain reminds me of Timothy Gilbert. As a man, he was worthy of high eulogy; as a philanthropist, he has won higher praise; but it is his Christianity that crowds up through his manhood and through his philanthropy, and to-day attracts the notice of mankind.

CHAPTER IV.

HIS MARRIAGE. — THE TREMONT TEMPLE ENTERPRISE. — NATHANIEL COLVER.

LESS than five years by thirty days after his arrival in Boston, he took to wife Mary Wetherbee, who was born in Ashburnham, Mass., July 7, 1796. Their only child, Mary Eunice, was born in Massachusetts, June 8, 1827, and afterwards became the wife of his partner in business and steadfast friend, Major William H. Jameson.

Miss Wetherbee possessed many remarkable traits of character. She was cheerful, and filled her home with sunshine. She was talented, and exerted a marked influence upon the circle in which she moved. She was benevolent and philanthropic to an extraordinary extent. Her footstep was a familiar sound as she climbed the garret stairways bearing food or medicine to the poor and sick. She was a felt power in the church and in the community. Her hand bound up the wounds of many a scarred slave, and supplied the wants of many a half-famished fugitive. The home of Timothy Gilbert was for years the station of the underground railroad in Boston. Men who were known to be true to liberty, in Hartford and elsewhere, relate that the slaves that passed through were all booked for No. 2 Beach Street. Sometimes as many as half a dozen of a night found shelter, friends, and comfort beneath that hospitable roof. A man cannot keep such a home unless the wife is willing. Mary Wetherbee Gilbert was ever willing, and the blessings of those ready to perish came to her in rich abundance.

She was devotedly pious, and shared with her husband his trials and his joys, and labored in the cause of Christ and humanity with pleasure to herself and with profit to those about her.

They went to keeping house in May, 1826. Early in 1829 he dissolved partnership with E. R. Currier, and commenced business alone in some lofts now occupied by John Putnam, but vacated by John Osborne in 1829.

The ten years that follow were passed in the quiet discharge of duties incident to the position he occupied in the church and in the world. His relations to the church in Charles Street, though in the main pleasant, induced him to seek a more congenial atmosphere, where he might give expression to his anti-slavery opinions. It is said, that when he contemplated uniting with Federal Street, there was a feeling of opposition on the part of some of the members because of his ultra views. Soon after his uniting with the church, he filled his pew with colored people. No one objected. Soon he became satisfied with the views of the church, and during his brief sojourn he pursued a course that endeared him to the membership, and secured, for the free place of worship he went out to establish, their sympathy and aid. In a letter addressed to the Tremont Street Church, September 3, 1852, he alludes to the supposition that it was his devotion to the anti-slavery reform which led him to take his stand, and says, "I came out from another church to aid in the formation of a free Baptist Church in Boston, not from any ill feeling towards those I left, nor wholly from a desire to carry out what I believed, and still believe, to be the principles of the Bible regarding slavery, intemperance, and other evils in the church of Christ; but my ultimate object, and without which I should not have been likely to have undertaken the enterprise, was to open in the city a centrally located house of worship, with free seats, on some self-supporting plan, where all, whatever might be their condition or circumstances in life, might have an opportunity to hear the gospel and enjoy the means of grace."

It was not then for political reasons, or even for the purpose of promoting any special reform, that he came out to enter upon this work. Boston churches were crowded. The pulpit was alive to the questions of the hour, and many of the churches were enjoying precious revivals.

Then, as now, a vast multitude were unreached. It was difficult to obtain sittings for strangers, and especially for the poor, in the houses of God. He longed to see the rich and poor meet together on a common level in the sanctuary, and so he conceived of the plan, which, if carried out, would make such a place largely self-sustaining. Hence he said, "I did this, having in view the fact that several other unsuccessful attempts had been made in New York and Boston.

"That fact, probably more than any other, led me, in order to prevent a failure, and have any reasonable hope of success, to seek for a place where the income of the property would in part, if not altogether, pay for itself — meet the current expenses of keeping the same in repair, support preaching so far as it was safe to do so, secure an active and efficient church, and in the end, if possible, have something to provide for the wants of the poor, of which such a church and congregation would be likely chiefly to consist." This he declares to have been his original purpose, and to have stated it to individuals and to the church without provoking any objections. With this object in view his mind was directed to the estate on which the Boston Museum now stands, and also to another site at the corner of Court and Sudbury Streets, both for sale. It was his custom — so he relates — frequently to go out at night in the hope of resting a weary brain and giving loose rein to his desires and longings for a free house of worship into which he might welcome the poor. At these times he would take long walks through the deserted streets. On one of these occasions, while oppressed and burdened with the condition of the young mechanics and apprentices, and also of the great crowd of strangers without a Sabbath home, he was walking down School Street, having just passed Tremont Theatre, when, suddenly impressed with the mission of such an establishment as the charter of Tremont Temple contemplates, he stopped, and retraced his steps, and stood in front of the old theatre. It was the noon of night. The bells were striking. The streets were silent. He bared his head and took his vow, offering a prayer for guidance.

Immediately he took steps to ascertain what was

required to make the purchase. To his surprise he found that for twelve thousand five hundred feet of land in the heart of Boston, covered by a building, substantially built, with a marble front and solid brick walls, the small sum of fifty-five thousand dollars would suffice to secure the property. He regarded the fact that capitalists should have failed to take it as a remarkable providence in his favor. Though the church was feeble in pecuniary strength, so that by many it was thought presumptuous to make the attempt, though many of the newspapers intimated that we should fail after the work was begun, which, considering the magnitude of the undertaking and our real strength, was not surprising; yet the Lord was on our side, and by his signal interpositions turned back the shafts of our enemies, and in several instances caused that which was intended to embarrass us to turn out for the advancement of the object. In this way, and not by our skill, or wisdom, or strength, the work was accomplished. It was the Lord's work, and it is marvellous in our eyes. There is a secret history which deserves to be uncovered. Few know into what straits and difficulties he was led by this undertaking. He records the fact that it was only by divine favor almost miraculously manifested, that the property now known as the Tremont Temple estate, is prospectively secured to the cause of Christ.

The following letter serves to throw light upon this portion of history: —

WASHINGTON, D. C., October 1, 1865.

DEAR BRO. FULTON: My first acquaintance with Mr. Gilbert was in 1840, when the First Baptist Free church (as it was then called) worshipped in Julian Hall, at the corner of Milk and Congress Streets, Boston. Mr. Gilbert was one of the original members of the church, and took a deep interest in its welfare and success. He was fully impressed with the importance of there being at least one place of worship in Boston with free seats, where all persons, whether rich or poor, without distinction of color or condition, could take a seat where they pleased, and have the gospel preached to them in its purity. He felt that such a place was needed in Boston, especially for the large class of floating population of young persons, male and female, who were not regular attendants at any church, but who might be induced to attend if the seats were free. To the accomplishment of this object he devoted much of his time, and of the means which his success in business had enabled him to accumulate, recognizing, as he always did, that plain principle of Christian duty (too often practically denied by many professed Christians), that all the property God, in his providence, places in our hands, is to be used as his, and not as our own; and that, as his stewards, we are accountable to him for the use of our time, and the means committed to our care.

Soon after the removal of our place of worship from Milk Street to the corner of Tremont and Bromfield Streets, Mr. Gilbert became deeply impressed with the importance of securing an eligible lot of land upon which to erect a large audience-room, capable of seating the thousands who were wandering around the streets and the Common on the Sabbath, but few of whom could be seated in the small hall occupied by us, and which was crowded to excess.

At this time I was his confidential clerk, and a member of the same church with him, and had, perhaps, a better opportunity than any one else of knowing his anxiety on the subject, and the immense amount of thought and labor which he prayerfully devoted to the accomplishment of the object which he believed God required should be accomplished.

Among other sites examined was the one now occupied by Kimball's Museum, on Tremont Street. The property was then owned by Hon. John C. Gray. After Mr. Gilbert had personally surveyed the land himself, and ascertained how large a hall could be built upon it, he went into a careful estimate of what an appropriate building would cost, and how much income might be obtained from the stores under the hall.

He then obtained from Mr. Gray his terms for the land, and a refusal of it for a certain length of time. He held frequent consultations with Deacon Simon G. Shipley, Thomas Gould, and William S. Damrell, all of whom were true friends of the enterprise, and had the fullest confidence in Mr. Gilbert's judgment and purity of motives, and were always ready to aid him to the extent of their ability. Just as matters were assuming a shape which seemed to warrant the purchase of the property, other parties commenced negotiating for the same, and Mr. Gray wrote a note to Mr. Gilbert, withdrawing his offer to sell on the terms he had before given. Mr. Gilbert was sadly disappointed, and endeavored to induce Mr. Gray to consent to his former terms, but without success.

About this time the owners of the Tremont Theatre

advertised that building for sale. Mr. Gilbert immediately made a thorough examination of that property, and consulted with the three persons I have before named, also with Deacon Samuel Hill, of South Boston, another true friend of the enterprise. Many a night have I spent with Mr. Gilbert, till near midnight, making estimates as to what it would cost to remodel the building, and what income could be reasonably expected from the stores and lettings of the halls.

Just at this time Mr. Gilbert met with an obstacle which gave him considerable anxiety. Upon consulting with his then partner in business, he found that, although he wished the object success, and was willing to do all he thought reasonable to accomplish it, he was fearful that it would take so much of Mr. Gilbert's time, and of the means of the firm, that it might seriously interfere with their business; and therefore he hesitated to give his consent. I well recollect the conversation he had with his partner on the subject, and it ended by his saying to him, "Well, think and pray over the matter to-night, and let me know in the morning your decision." In the morning his partner said, "I cannot see my way clear to consent." "Well," said Mr. Gilbert, "I have prayed much over the subject, and think God requires me to do it; and if I cannot do it with you as my partner, I must do it without your being my partner."

Finding that Mr. Gilbert felt that his duty to God required him to do it, his partner then consented.

Having been thus relieved by the consent of his partner, what was his surprise, on taking up the morning paper, to find, among the items of news, that the

Tremont Theatre had been sold to the Massachusetts Charitable Mechanics' Association, and that the papers had been passed the day before. His disappointment was extreme, that after all his labors and anxiety, God had seemed again to block his way to success. I suggested to him that possibly the report in the papers might not be true, and, at his request, I went immediately to see the treasurer of the Theatre Corporation, who informed me that a bargain *had* been made with the Mechanics' Association, and he had considered it settled, but that the previous afternoon, when he met the representatives of the Association to pass the papers, he found there was a misunderstanding, the Mechanics' Association claiming that the chandeliers and gas-fixtures were to be included in the purchase, while the Theatre Corporation insisted that they were not to be included, and that this small matter only had prevented the consummation of the sale. He said he had no doubt the Association would, upon reflection, yield their claim to the gas-fixtures, but that he was *now* at liberty to make the sale to any one else.

I returned at once, and informed Mr. Gilbert, and we immediately went with Messrs. Shipley, Gould, Damrell, and, I think, Deacon Clement Drew, and had the papers drawn up and signed, made the required payment, and consummated the purchase that day.

About this time I became a partner in business with Mr. Gilbert and Mr. Safford, and Mr. Gilbert devoted nearly his whole time to superintending the remodelling of the building. For nearly a year his mind was engrossed and his time spent at the building; and again, when the old Tremont Temple was destroyed, he devoted all his time, and the entire credit of the firm, in rebuilding the present structure, performing an amount of labor, and assuming pecuniary responsibilities, known to but few at the time.

I have thus hastily and briefly stated a few facts, which I thought, perhaps, may not have come to your notice.

His other services in the church, and his successful efforts to prevent the Temple from being sold out of the control of the Baptist denomination, are, no doubt, well known to you.

Thank God, he lived to see two objects accomplished, for which he had long labored and prayed, viz., our beloved country redeemed from the curse of slavery, and the Tremont Temple enterprise a permanent success.

Yours, truly,

WM. H. JAMESON.

Mr. G.'s consecration to Christ was only equalled by his reliance upon Christ. Frequently, when his way was hedged up and he could see no hope of deliverance, when he wanted money to meet his obligations and keep the Temple from interfering with his legitimate business, with a faith second neither to that which characterized Elijah when he prayed for fire to descend from heaven, nor that which distinguished Müller when he spread out the wants of his orphans, he has been known to shut himself up in his room, and abstain from food, from society, from family, and from business, that he might uncover the interests of the cause of Christ, spread them out before God, and cry for help. When he gained the assurance of victory he would descend with a smile from his mount of prayer, and was never known to be disappointed in results. It is a fact that burdens steady the lone column. Is it not possible that these trials, coming in the midst of anti-slavery excitements, held him as with hooks of steel to the cause espoused and to the church? "I am sure," said he, "that no one who has gone to God as I have, and received such manifest tokens of the divine favor, would now dare abandon the undertaking that had been so signally favored, while there was any reasonable prospect left that it could be carried through. I could, with as little compunctions of conscience, set my face against the church of Christ, and advocate infidelity, as to turn against the enterprise in which I had so manifestly seen God's favor." He was then in the prime of a healthy manhood, had enough of persistency and stick-to-ativeness about him to follow up his convictions, and so the conception which dropped into his mind as a thought from God, grew until he came to believe in the possibility of furnishing, in the centre of Boston, a place of worship free and accessible to all, which might win the present beautiful appellation of "The Stranger's Sabbath Home." The plan was simple and unique. It was no other than to take a building of sufficient capacity, fit it up for stores and offices, the rent of which should provide for current expenses and repairs, and at the same time, when the debt was removed, furnish a mission fund to be used in providing for the destitute at home and abroad.

The Tremont Street Church was formed of eighty-two members, April 18, 1839, and for twelve years was served by Nathaniel Colver as pastor. The number added by baptism and letter during the year 1840 was ninety; in 1841, thirty; in 1842, one hundred and twenty-six.

The retrospect from this point is delightful. When the project was started, and the foundations of this enterprise were laid, the cause of Christ, in Boston, was going on from conquest to conquest. Baldwin Place Church was crowded under the ministry of Rev. Baron Stow, D. D. Rollin H. Neale, a young man, began his ministry in 1837, and in 1838 there was not a seat to be found in that thronged sanctuary where waiting crowds hung spell-bound, and listened with delight to an oratory which then as now glows with the love of Christ. Charles Street was at court end, crowded with the hundreds who admired the courtly Daniel Sharp, whose praise is yet in all the churches, while the Hall in Boylston Street in which Robert Turnbull preached, and the house in Federal Street in which the eloquent Howard Malcom had ministered, waited with a splendid congregation to welcome a worthy successor, which they found in William Hague. Then it was Nathaniel Colver came. He was fresh from the country. He was impulsive, bold, eloquent, thoroughly honest, somewhat eccentric. He was a power because he was a man of God. He swayed a mighty influence. Born in Orwel, Vermont, May 10, 1794, the son of a minister of Christ, who was noted as a self-made man, strong and lucid in the exhibition of truth, attributing his conversion to the accumulating power of God's word, long and intense thought, attended by the Holy Ghost; from a child accustomed to strong religious impressions, the result of a pious mother's influence, when the Spirit of God wrought his work in his heart, there was a change produced. He loved to describe it. He had been to an evening meeting. He was on his way home. His burden was too heavy for him to bear. He went into the woods, and there, like Jacob by the brook, wrestled for deliverance. It came at the break of day, and he arose a new man in Christ Jesus. When he came to Boston, parties were ranging for a desperate conflict. Possessed of a clear and logical mind, endowed with a lively imagination, with great powers of argumentation, a ready debater, perfectly fearless in the enunciation of truth, — he took at once a foremost position, and became a champion of the oppressed, and a leading advocate of Temperance and of Reform.

Two letters addressed to "Dear brother Gilbert," dated April 10, and May 10, 1839, reveal the heart of the man, his attachment to his flock in Greenwich, N. Y., and at the same time his fondness for the work in Boston. He was "bound in the spirit." He asks the church to meet him at the throne of grace at half past nine o'clock each evening. "I feel as if it would be a pleasure to me to stand up in one of your little parlor meetings and preach from the text, 'What is thy beloved more than any other beloved,' or from David's words, 'Whom have I in heaven but thee? and there is none upon earth that I desire beside thee.'

'What wondrous grace in Jesus reigns
To love and cleanse us from our stains,
That with his own best robe adorns,
And puts a comeliness on worms!'

"I love David and Solomon because they spoke so well of my God. I admire that a religion so old as to have been their companion, can be so fresh and new as it appears to me to-night. David's offering was a broken heart. The fires of divine love consumed it upon the altar. O Lord, help me to lay my heart, all broken, upon the same altar, and let the same fire come down from heaven and embrace it."

Breathing this spirit of consecration to the service of Christ, he came to Boston and was installed as pastor of the First Free Church, afterwards known as the Tremont Street Church, and now by the union of the Baptist Church in Merrimac Street with the Tremont Street Baptist Church, the Union Temple Baptist Church, on September 15, 1839, in the First Baptist Church. For three months the church met in Tremont Row, one year in Congress Hall, and afterwards until the completion of the Temple, in a Hall under the Museum building, corner of Tremont and Bromfield Streets.

In Nathaniel Colver, Deacon Gilbert found his counterpart. They were unlike in many particulars, but were admirably adapted to work together. Mr. Gilbert was extremely anxious that his pastor should be stripped of all infirmities, that, fetterless and free, he might pursue his work for God and souls.

The story of Mr. C. being cured from the use of tobacco deserves mention. When he came to Boston he was an inveterate user of the weed. It grieved and tried Deacon Gilbert. We have noticed the deacon's adherence to a principle, and the means he used to press his point. One day he gave his pastor a five-dollar bill, and told him to hand it back when he recommenced the use of the narcotic. By some strange mishap Mr. Colver lost the bill. Then came back the desire to smoke with increased strength. Mr. C. took another bill, and carried it to the deacon, laying it down, and saying, "I have concluded to resume the use of tobacco." Those who are familiar with the deacon will recall with what moderation he would turn around, take up the bill, and express his sorrow. While looking at the money his black eye flashed. A thought illumined his face. He perceived that his pastor was in his power, and that he was master of the situation. Quietly and calmly he remarked, handing it back, "*This is not the bill I gave you*, and before you can smoke with my consent you must return that one." "But I have lost it," exclaimed the pastor. "Can't help it," replied the deacon. Two determined men met and stood face to face. Timothy Gilbert, in such a cause, was immovable. The search was renewed and prosecuted for a time, but at last principle came to his aid, and the mastery was gained, and Mr. Colver became a strong anti-tobacco advocate.

Mr. Gilbert would not allow the use of tobacco in his house without making it unpleasant for those who indulged in the degrading practice, and he exerted a strong influence towards weeding out this cursed poison from the ranks of the ministry, as many others can bear witness besides the first pastor of the Tremont Street Church.

As has been intimated, the church were accustomed to gather for prayer in Mr. Gilbert's parlors, where the poorest was welcomed as well as those capacitated to share his burdens. That little company has been thinned by death; yet a few remain who remember those seasons of refreshing from on high, and each and all speak of the happiness of him who placed his talents, property, and time upon the altar of sacrifice. The close and pungent preaching of the pastor delighted and fed him. The cry, "I am wounded," which frequently greeted their ears as some lost soul sought Christ, was to him like the song of the turtle and the singing of birds — the precursor of the coming of the Lord. He carried his principles into his business and into his pleasures. He was not a companionable man. He was full of energy and push, and made the indolent uneasy in his presence, and by his life and speech evidenced very little respect for those who desired rest. His wife shared his sympathy, and had wonderful control over his restless spirit. She was a helpmeet indeed. Here is a glimpse of a meeting sketched by her hand in a letter dated May 5, 1840: "Beloved Husband: I have just received your kind and affectionate letter. Although I have since heard from you, through Mr. Safford, yet to receive a letter from you is very grateful to my feelings. Every word is like apples of gold in pictures of silver. I expect you would like to hear from the church, and so I will give you an account of the Friday evening meeting. Five candidates related their experience. For that reason there was not time for a covenant meeting. Sabbath day, Mr. Colver baptized at South Boston. In the afternoon Mr. Colver gave the right hand of fellowship to about thirty. We had a very precious season. Surely the Lord is good to us; let his praise be ever upon our lips." On the same sheet is a note, written by his daughter, which shows the child's heart, and indicates the child's love and confidence. "Dear Father: I received your kind letter this afternoon, and read it with interest. I wish I could love the Saviour as well as I do you; but I can't feel as I ought. If I try to think about anything serious, my thoughts will wander to something else, and I can't keep my mind on it. I wish you would pray for me, that my thoughts may be kept upon the Saviour. I want to see you very much, indeed; it seems as though you had been gone a month. Please write me another letter before you come home, if it is convenient." How truthfully such letters mirror the home life of a man! Two days later the wife writes, "The time seems very long since you left, but I hope to see you now soon. I should like to hear of your prosperity, but I hope neither of us will be over-anxious about temporal concerns. If our souls prosper, and are in health, we shall be happy, whether in prosperity or adversity. In your letter you mentioned that you thought of the church in the hour of prayer. I can assure you, you are not forgotten by them. At the close of the meeting, all ask when I expect you home, and exclaim, 'How we miss him!' And Mr. Colver said, last evening, 'It made a big hole in Boston to have you gone.' I hope we shall not think too much of the creature, and forget the Creator — the great fountain from whence all our blessings flow. It gives me pleasure to learn of your access to the throne of grace. It must be very sweet, after the toils of the day, to retire alone, and commune with your heavenly Father; to feel that we have a Saviour, that careth for us, on whom we can roll all our cares, and tell him every joy and every sorrow; one who has said, not a hair of your head shall fall to the ground without his notice. May our love for the precious Saviour increase every day, until our hearts are filled with his love, and we can tread the world beneath our feet." The thirteen-year-old daughter adds, in her usual place, "Dear Father: I want to see you very much, and give you a kiss." This letter also furnishes the intimation, that Mr. Colver is going to London, to attend the great convention, and reveals the way the money was raised, when Sewing Societies and Emancipation Societies united in sending their fearless representative to the world's great mart, to vindicate the cause of oppressed humanity.

CHAPTER V.

REV. JACOB KNAPP — THE BAPTIST CAUSE IN BOSTON IN 1840. — THE CHARACTER OF THE EVANGELIST, AND HIS WORK IN NEW BEDFORD, PROVIDENCE, AND BOSTON. — LETTER FROM MR. KNAPP, SHOWING THE PART BORNE IN THE WORK BY MR. GILBERT.

IN 1840 the Bowdoin Square Church was formed, with one hundred and forty members, and with the erudite and scholarly Robert W. Cushman for pastor. The churches of Boston at that time were largely led by young men with whose names fame has long been familiar. In the pulpit of the First Church was Rollin H. Neale; Baron Stow ministered in Baldwin Place, William Hague in Federal Street, Daniel Sharp in Charles Street, Robert Turnbull in Boylston Street, and Nathaniel Colver in Tremont Street. Dr. Neale had been but a few years out of the seminary, and was noted even then for his eloquence and power. The church in Baldwin Place was thronged, and the ardent and impulsive Stow thrilled the hearts of waiting multitudes. William Hague was in the midst of a powerful work in Federal Street. Then, as now, he was planning large things for the cause of his Master, and reaped with no sparing hand. At this period, so opportune for the churches, the cloud appeared over New Bedford, and the sound of an abundance of rain was heard in various portions of New England. On the 5th day of June, Rev. Jacob Knapp unfurled in New Bedford the banner of the cross, in sight of the ship-masters and sailors of that city by the sea. Rev. Henry Jackson, pastor of the church, in a letter to the Taunton Association, says, "For seven weeks, in the midsummer months, the people met him in the house of God thrice daily, except when detained by ill health." Days of fasting, humiliation, and prayer were observed. Incessant and importunate prayer continually ascended to God. A few persons indulged a hope, but the great mass of the unconverted were unaffected. The church was confident that so much prayer could not be lost. They held to the promises of God's word, and pleaded for the honor of Jehovah, the reputation of the cross of Christ, and the value of souls, that God would not withhold his Spirit. Many obstacles existed. The heat of the weather, the pressure of business, the shortness of the evenings, and, above all, the infidelity of the people, and the unbelief of Christians, seemed for a season to baffle every effort. At last the Spirit came down with mighty power, and hundreds crowded the rooms of prayer, deeply in earnest to know what they must do to be saved. The entire choir were converted. Baptismal scenes were indescribably solemn when evangelist and pastor buried willing disciples at the same time in the likeness of Christ. About three hundred and fifty were hopefully converted to God. This meeting introduced Jacob Knapp to New England.

He was then forty-two years of age. He possessed transcendent abilities as an orator. He was Christ's lieutenant, and knew how to get his Captain's companies into line, and prepare them for action. He believed in a personal God and in a personal devil. Like Luther, he was a man of faith and a man of war.

Born in Otsego, Otsego County, N. Y., December 7, 1799, the son of a farmer, his parents members of the Episcopal church, he was early indoctrinated into the forms. When converted to God, he was led not by a minister or a church, but by the Spirit and word of God, to be a Baptist. He was immersed by Rev. Daniel Robertson, in Masonville, Delaware County, N. Y., in 1819. He entered the literary and theological institution of Hamilton, N. Y., in 1822, and graduated in 1825. For eight years he preached as a pastor, after which he devoted himself to the work of an evangelist. Of him, as a man of God, there have been, and will be, a diversity of views. He was bold, uncompromising, and determined. His preaching would please those who wanted the devil's kingdom stirred up, while it would displease those who longed for peace and quiet. Of his general character there was but one opinion; but of the measures he employed, and the course he pursued, in these meetings, various and conflicting opinions were entertained. Fear and hope alternately preponderated, until all came to the full conviction that one possessing such pure and elevated piety, and governed so generally by the motives of Christ, would not be suffered widely to err. Confidence in him and his measures was confirmed. These results were constantly substantiated by the effects produced upon the multitudes who thronged the house. Men and women of established character experienced by this instrumentality the power of the gospel. The work increased in interest and execution, by the same means, after he had gone — a fact demonstrating that God had owned and put his seal upon them. Anxious seats had been complained of, and by the church hitherto dreaded. At last, though no importance was attached to the bench, yet it was viewed as a means by which hundreds have been brought to a decision in religion. Elder Knapp preached the gospel in its simplicity and power. He hesitated not to expose sin in every form, and strove mainly for the awakening and perfecting of the saints and the conversion of sinners. In his departure he bore abundant proofs of the confidence and respect of the pastor, the church, and the community, and was commended to the churches as one who had given evidence of being designated by the great Head of the church to the work of an evangelist.

From New Bedford, Mr. Knapp went to Providence, on the 19th of September, to the help of Rev. John Dowling, D. D., where it is thought over four hundred were led to Christ. It was while in Providence that he was prosecuted for referring to the character of an individual who had disturbed the meeting. The action served to call attention to him, and induced Dr. Dowling to give this wholesome advice, which is worthy of general acceptance: "*Do not distract his mind by telling him any of the floating gossip with which probably your city will be filled during his stay among you. Tell him nothing which you may hear, except what may have a tendency to strengthen his hands and encourage his heart in the work in which he is engaged.'*—I am convinced that but few men live so near to God, and possess so much of all that is excellent in the Christian character, as brother Knapp. May the Lord help me and all my ministering brethren to drink as deep into the spirit of Christ, and hold as sweet communion with God, as that dear brother!" Rev. T. C. Jameson, who within ten weeks baptized one hundred and twelve converts, added his testimony to the fervor and power of this man of God. In Providence there was determined opposition to his efforts, on the part of several distinguished ministers. On the other hand, a document, speaking of him in the highest praise, was signed by over three thousand individuals, and forwarded to Boston, where an effort was being made to destroy his influence. On or about the 1st of January, 1842, he began his labors with the First Church, Rev. Rollin H. Neale, pastor, and preached there in the afternoon, in the evening at Baldwin Place, Rev. Baron Stow, pastor. On Monday, January 9, Mr. Knapp commenced at Bowdoin Square Church, where he preached both afternoon and evening. It was while here that he met his fiercest oppositions. Mobs gathered about Bowdoin Square as they gathered in the olden time about the synagogue in Lystra, and would have stoned Jacob Knapp, and have dragged him through the city, as the Jews persuaded the people of Lystra to do unto the apostle to the Gentiles. Never did chieftain bear himself more bravely, never did martyr walk more in humble reliance upon the promises of a covenant-keeping God, than did this fearless preacher. Citizens were stirred by his appeal and awed by his sublime courage. William Ellery Channing said, concerning him, "Let the minister alone; a man who can stir Boston like that will do good."

Day after day the excitement grew more fierce and intense. At length it was reported throughout the city that Mayor Chapman had said that the preacher was imprudent, and might take the consequences of his own conduct. Immediately Rev. William Hague, though not a supporter of his measures, called upon the mayor, and informed him of the report, saying that the occasion made its appeal to every lover of religious liberty, and in such an emergency he should feel it to be his duty to stand beside the preacher, and share the consequences. The mayor replied, "Sir, the report is not true, and all the power I have at my command shall be concentrated at Bowdoin Square to-night in defence of freedom of speech." The crowds were dispersed.

To the honor of the secular press be it said that with united voice they sustained the action of the mayor, and supported the ambassador of Christ through the terrible ordeal.

There was on hesitation on the part of his friends. The church at Baldwin Place unanimously invited Mr. Knapp to preach in their meeting-house. The tide continued to flow in, and indications of the divine approval abounded. The spiritual strength of Mr. Knapp seemed literally renewed. He fired no blank cartridges, but delivered broadsides at close range into the ranks of the foe. The opposition roused him and encouraged him. The attendance upon theatres waned, that upon churches increased. On February 9, 1842, the "Reflector" says, "It is our privilege to do something more than merely report progress. The work has now attained to a degree of prevalence and power that renders it utterly impossible for us to convey to our more distant readers an adequate conception of what God is permitting his people to witness and enjoy in Boston. Every day brings to light facts and scenes of the most thrilling interest. Among the converts, which now amount to hundreds, there are persons from every class and of every description of moral character—old men with thin and silvered locks, with deeply-furrowed cheeks, and voices tremulous and feeble, who were long since given up by their friends as hopeless cases, are, like little children, praying and weeping, and talking of the infinitude of God's mercy and the love of Christ; and young men glowing with energy and ambition, strong with health and hope, are proclaiming, with apostolic fervor, the truths which to some are a stumbling-block, and to others foolishness; children are in many instances rejoicing over their parents' conversion, and in many others, parents are blessing God for the conversion of their children. A family in which father and mother and five adult children were converted were led to Christ through the instrumentality of a single young lady. Her importunity led them to the meetings; her kind and correct endeavors dissuaded them from dropping the subject or avoiding the influence which was now creeping over them. She rested not till God and conscience had done their work, and the souls she loved were loved of Heaven.

"On Tuesday evening of last week, brother Knapp

made 'Universalism' the theme of his discourse, and for two hours and a half held a vast and crowded auditory in almost breathless silence, while he tore up the foundations of the system, and scattered the whole fabric to the winds. Never did we hear such an array of facts — authentic, astounding, withering facts. We thought that even his Satanic Majesty himself, had he appeared there as a Universalist, must have quailed under them, and hung his head in shame."

A young man, a member of Mr. Skinner's congregation, led by curiosity, found his way to Baldwin Place. Strong in the faith of Universalism, he listened with candor, as one inquiring after truth; and the result was, that Mr. Knapp swept away every vestige of his Universalism, and, to use his own language, "took away every shingle and clapboard of the building — left nothing but the falling rafters, exposing his naked soul to the peltings of the pitiless storm." The revival was characterized by the apparent genuineness of the conversions. The converts exhibited a clear understanding of the evil of sin, the holiness of God's laws, the doctrine of justification by faith, and the necessity of entire consecration to God — topics on which Mr. Knapp dwelt with great frequency and power. Though some of the ministers treated Mr. Knapp coolly, the majority of the churches were heart and soul with him.

On the first Sabbath in February, forty-two united with the First Church, fourteen with Bowdoin Square, nineteen with Baldwin Place, and twenty-two with Tremont Street.

On March 2 this announcement is made under the

head of "Theatres:" "The friends of morality and religion will rejoice to learn that the great theatre of Boston, the Tremont, is closed, and that noble granite edifice is offered for sale, and is likely to be converted into a house of worship. At the conclusion of a late entertainment, the manager announced that the theatre would be closed, and stated that within the last three months they had lost ten thousand dollars by keeping it open." The rush was in a different direction. The churches were thronged, and Mr. Knapp went from place to place, like a general on the field of battle, giving aid where needed. A writer in the "New York Evangelist" says of him, "He preaches in his own style, saying some things that are not in good taste, yet no doubt doing execution." A professor in one of our theological schools attended upon his preaching a whole Sabbath since he has been here, and on being asked his opinion, replied, "He is a man of genius and power, and though his preaching is not always in good taste, yet no thief, or profane swearer, or drunkard, or adulterer, can sit and listen to him a great while without feeling that the constable is after him."

The work goes on in increasing power. New and striking cases of conviction are daily occurring among persons of every faith, and class, and character; wholesale dealers in ardent spirits have yielded to the spirit of God, and abandoned the cursed traffic. A large distiller was found beside a vender among the inquirers. Baptisms are occurring in the different churches every Sabbath, and the work is spreading through the commonwealth. March 9 the "Puritan" has taken sides against Mr. Knapp, and three eminent divines of the straitest sect declare "the sentiments of Mr. Knapp are substantially sound, *so far as they go*, but his violation of good taste is the great secret of his notoriety."

The "Reflector" speaks of Sabbath, March 6, as furnishing a scene upon which angels would look with delight. "Picture to yourself a crowded sanctuary, with its long centre aisle occupied from end to end with a dense double column of 'new recruits' to the army, fighting under the banners of our King, and then receiving, one after another, the significant pledge of Christian affection, and passing round, one to the right hand and another to the left, until the last young soldier was greeted, and all duly enrolled with the sacramental host of God's elect. The work has been more powerful in the First Church, during the last week, than at any time before. It seems as if not a single soul among them all was to be left in a state of unreconciliation to God. Baptisms reported: First Church, fifty-eight; Baldwin Place, fifty-two; Free Church, forty; Bowdoin Square, twenty-seven; Federal Street, twenty-eight; Boylston Street, twenty-four; Charles Street, six; Independent, nineteen. Notwithstanding these results, the "New England Puritan" ridicules the labors of Mr. Knapp, saying, "The operations after the sermons are more objectionable than anything in the sermons themselves." Calling forward to the anxious seat is characterized by declaring that "the congregation is put into a rambling state and some fifteen minutes of confusion." "Against such machinery, so productive of wholesale delusion, so destructive to the modesty becoming women and children, and so calculated to lead all impenitent men to the conclusion that religion is promoted by trick and artifice, we feel bound to enter our solemn protest;" and all this because Mr. Knapp, at the conclusion of the sermon, was accustomed to come down from the pulpit and exhort the impenitent to come to Christ, and converts to tell what God had done for their souls. The third week of March closed his labors in Boston, with the blessings of thousands ready to perish resting upon him, and following him to Lowell, his next field of labor.

In accordance with the request of the leading citizens of Boston, he repeated the Temperance Sermon in Marlboro' Chapel, which, two years before, in Baltimore, led to the reformation of J. H. W. Hawkins, and initiated the Washingtonian reform. At the conclusion of the address, all who had signed the total abstinence pledge, or were determined to sign it, were asked to rise; and the whole of that immense assemblage sprang to their feet. It was a thrilling scene, and proved the potency of the religion of Christ to promote a spirit of reform.

The time of his sojourn drew to a close. In the "Reflector" of March 23 there was a description of the closing scenes. "The mornings of Thursday and Friday, March 17 and 18, were occupied with meetings devoted to expressions of gratitude for the distinguishing mercies of Heaven. These meetings were full of interest. Thursday evening he preached to converts in Bowdoin Square. Friday afternoon he preached to Christians at Baldwin Place; and though it was a week day, and in the hurry of spring, such was the enthusiasm, that every standing place in the house was taken, and multitudes went away. In the evening he preached to the impenitent at Bowdoin Square, and the solemn service was concluded with the parting and farewell of those parties who had labored with him."

The preceding statements help to an understanding of the letter written by the evangelist after the lapse of nearly a quarter of a century. "My first acquaintance with Deacon Timothy Gilbert was in the close of 1841 and the beginning of 1842. I boarded in his family a portion of the three months' campaign in that city, during which thousands were converted to God, and the Tremont Theatre was wound up and soon converted into a place of divine worship. God, through my agency, wound up the theatre, and through the agency of brother Gilbert, converted it into a house of worship. He entered into the great and never-to-be-forgotten work of divine grace with all his powers of body and mind. For many days he arose in the morning before daylight, harnessed his horse and buggy, and took me to South Boston, where I found a crowded house waiting with profound stillness and solemnity to hear the word of life (for the religious interest in Boston then was such as to fill any house at any hour of the night). This dear, lamented brother would then accompany me, at ten o'clock A. M., to the anxious room, where we labored with great and overwhelming interest for two hours; then again I preached at two o'clock P. M., and again at half past seven P. M., and wound up, at ten o'clock

P. M., with a precious inquiry meeting, and brother Gilbert was the most of the time weeping and praying by my side, ready to every good word and work.

"At one time he called all of his workmen together in his parlor, and requested me to address them upon the necessity of securing the salvation of their souls. But I soon found that his appeals were more powerful than mine. He told them that he did not consider the capital in his possession *his*. It all belonged to God, and he was carrying on business for God and the good of the world, and he wished them all to attend the meetings and secure the salvation of their souls, and if any of them were in want of anything, to call upon him and their wants should be supplied. All were deeply affected, and some of them were speedily converted to God.

"In the winter of 1860, when laboring in Boston, I was made a welcome inmate of his family, both by himself and by his kind-hearted wife. At this time I found him the same warm-hearted Christian, governed, as formerly, by religious principles, regardless of public opinion, only desirous to know his Master's will, and ready to do it. At this time I baptized his two daughters, and we enjoyed many sweet and heavenly interviews together. But I perceived that the eighteen years which had intervened since our former association in the labors of the kingdom, had produced a marked change in my old friend, as was the case with Deacon William Hill, and many others. The vigor of his physical constitution was diminished, and his powers of endurance were not what they had been. The vast amount of his business, the embarrassed condition of his finances, and the great responsibilities which rested upon him, seemed too much for him longer to endure, and I was not surprised when the sad tidings reached my western home, that Deacon Timothy Gilbert was no more. Of him it may be said, 'Blessed are the dead which die in the Lord; they rest from their labors, and their works do follow them.'"

So much for the revival. Through that interesting period Timothy Gilbert was at the front. When mobs assailed them, he bared his head to the storm, and gloried in the reproach of Christ. He procured an elegant engraving of Mr. Knapp. He nursed him as he would a child when worn down with fatigue. That quiet home was the place to rest and recuperate. Other ministers and evangelists can testify to the revivifying influence exerted there. Mr. Gilbert was fond of talking about Mr. Knapp. When asked as to wherein lay the power of Mr. Knapp, he replied in his nearness to God, in his faith, in his ability in the pulpit, and in his generalship. It was Mr. Gilbert's custom to take down the texts, and to give a brief sketch of the sermon. It is possible to follow Mr. Knapp through the three months by these memoranda, to tell the texts used, and discover indications of the rise and growth of the interest. A description of Mr. Knapp as a preacher, and a report of one of his sermons, are preserved among his papers. In this description the secret of the evangelist's power is said to lie in the narrative nature of his discourses, and in the dramatic dress in which they are frequently clothed. He often introduced real or imaginary characters, acting and speaking in a manner appropriate to each. The text was in Acts xiii. 40, 41: "Beware, therefore, lest that come upon you which is spoken of in the prophets: Behold, ye despisers, and wonder and perish, for I work a work in your days, a work which ye shall in no wise believe, though a man declare it unto you." After some introductory remarks upon the danger and folly of despising the warnings and the operation of the Spirit of God, especially at the present time, when they are so remarkably manifest, he proceeded to specify instances of this great sin, and of its consequences, cited from the Old Testament. He began with Moses in Egypt, who showed his divine commission to Pharaoh, in the miracles he performed and in the judgments brought upon the land by Pharaoh's despising them, and refusing to liberate the Hebrews, whom he kept as slaves. This great monarch, said he, beheld and despised, wondered and perished. He also saw the Red Sea miraculously divide for their passage, and he, no doubt, "wondered" at so astonishing an event; but he "despised and perished;" he and his armies were overwhelmed and drowned in its waters. The preacher here introduced, in his peculiar manner, by way of parenthesis, the observation that Moses was an abolitionist. The Hebrews were slaves in Egypt, and he, by command of God, undertook to restore their freedom, to abolish their slavery, and to raise them to the rank of a flourishing and independent nation. In this, after great opposition, difficulty, and suffering, he finally, under God, succeeded.

He next alluded to the destruction of Sodom. Lot warned the wicked inhabitants of the consequences of their great sins. He finally predicted the destruction of the city and all the inhabitants, on a certain day, by fire and brimstone. They only laughed at the prediction. They called him a fool and fanatic. The Universalists gathered around him, and asked him if "he thought a kind and merciful God would destroy a whole city, men, women, and innocent children, in so barbarous a manner? No; they had a better opinion of God. He was not such a cruel, malicious, unmerciful being, delighting in the misery and ruin of the children he created." On the morning of the appointed day the sun rose in all his beauty and splendor; there was not a cloud to be seen in the whole heavens. The air was pure and serene, and there was never a fairer prospect of an uncommonly fine day. "Ah," said they to Lot, "what do you think of this? Does this look like a storm of fire and brimstone? You see now what nonsense you have been telling us." They "despised" him and his preaching. But by and by the air began to change, and became impure, the sky was overcast, the sun was obscured, and the heavens gathered blackness. These despisers began to "wonder;" they became alarmed. At length the thunderings and the lightnings commenced, and torrents of fire and brimstone were poured down upon this wicked and devoted city. Every soul perished, except Lot and his family, who departed in season to escape. Thus these sinful and depraved unbelievers "despised, and wondered, and perished."

Allusion was made to Noah and the building of the ark. He proclaimed the coming flood, and warned the people to prepare for it. He set an example by beginning to build an ark, and during the many years of his labor upon it, he ceased not to warn and advise all around him. But they would not believe him. They would, however, collect together, and look on, and wonder, and despise, and hold long conversations together. One would say, "Our neighbor, Noah, is a very good, kind, well-meaning man, and a good citizen, and it is a pity he should be led away by such strange notions." "Yes," said another, "he means well; he is pious, sincere, and benevolent, and talks to us, no doubt, in good faith; but he has got a strange kink in his head, and there is no getting it out of him. I'm afraid he will ruin himself in building this great, useless ship." "So am I," said a third; "he is not only honest and pious, but a man of excellent sense, and very shrewd in everything but this. But he is perfectly deranged about this bugbear of a flood, and I am afraid he will soon become perfectly insane. He is evidently a monomaniac, if nothing worse." "What a strange, inconsistent notion it is," said a fourth, "to think that God, just as he has got his new world well peopled, after so many years, will now destroy all he has done, render all his labor useless, and be obliged to begin again. No; God understands, and contrives, and foresees, better than all this." "Yes," said a fifth, "our neighbor is, in the main, a very good kind of a man, and I pity him. But I am afraid that, by this absurd fanaticism, he will not only injure himself, but that he will make hundreds of others equally insane, rendering them unhappy in themselves, and useless, if not burdensome, to their families, and to the community. I think it might be well to collect a mob in the night, set fire to his useless ark, and drive him away from this part of the country." Thus they beheld, and despised, and wondered, till the flood came — till the predictions of Noah were fulfilled, and the unbelieving people were all drowned.

These instances, with the descriptions and expressions, and novel and unexpected remarks, fixed the attention of a crowded audience through a long discourse. The application and conclusion were addressed to the conscience and the feelings, in reference to what he considered the wonderful operations of God then going on in the city. He warned all present not to oppose the work. He invited them to join in it, to repent and be converted, and save their own souls. But if they would not do this, let them not prevent others. "For if this counsel, or this work, be of men, it will come to nought; but if it be of God, ye cannot overthrow it; lest haply ye be found even to fight against God." "Beware, therefore, lest that come upon you which is spoken of in the prophets: Behold, ye despisers, and wonder, and perish."

Such preaching did good then, and will do good now. It brings out before the eye the pictures God's own hand had hung along the walls of the historic temple, for the instruction and guidance of the race. It made the word of God a living verity. There was no quibbling among the rank and file. The ministers vied with each other in helping forward the work. The church, as one man, sustained, by their presence, coöperation, and influence, the honored chieftain who went forth relying upon the promises of Jehovah.

As a result, all classes were moved. Each one worked over against his own house. Merchants worked with merchants, young men with young men, women of position with women of position. The Christian tree bent its branches downward, and spread its branches outward, and covered with its shadow vast multitudes. The bold and austere manner of the preacher, the terrible and scathing power used in exposing Universalism and kindred errors, his oddities, and yet remarkable flights of soul-stirring and soul-awing oratory, attracted immense multitudes, while the manner in which he was sustained by preacher and layman, the way they said 'Amen' to what was said and done, added to the sword he wielded, the weight and the authority of the entire church.

This was a most wonderful period in denominational history. The laity that upheld the hands of the ministry were unsurpassed in character, in talent, and in devotion. Every church was strong, because each church might, like the Sultan of the East, point to her stalwart men as the walls of her defence and the implements of conquest. It was at this period Daniel Safford introduced Rev. E. N. Kirk, D. D., to Boston. It was a remarkable happen-so, even if it were a happen-so, that Mr. Kirk followed Mr. Knapp so frequently. One was the John the Baptist, preaching repentance, and the other was the reaper. One was the blacksmith, the other the silversmith. Said Dr. Kirk, "I delighted to follow Mr. Knapp, because he stirred the conscience, and made a great number ready to listen to the truth, presented in a milder form. They were too mad to hear him, they were under too deep conviction to rest content; so many gladly came to listen to me who might have gone, unmoved, to perdition, had it not been for the sledge-hammer style of Mr. Knapp." For this reason he followed him, in Baltimore, in New Haven, and in Boston.

From this most delightful period of revival interest we must turn to a scene of conflict, which found its origin in the awakened conscience of the lovers of Christ. The life of Timothy Gilbert was interlaced with the life of the world in many ways. Follow the thread where you will, and it enables you to confront sterling worth, incorruptible honesty, and an unflinching adherence to what he deemed right towards God and man. The man who defended revivals, and who was the right-hand man of the evangelist, defended the slave, and for many years bore the burden and heat of the conflict.

CHAPTER VI.

ANTI-SLAVERY AGITATION IN THE CHURCH. — THE PROCEEDINGS OF THE MISSION BOARD AT BALTIMORE. — EXCITING DISCUSSION. — LETTER OF BARON STOW. — ORGANIZATION OF THE PROVISIONAL COMMITTEE. — TIMOTHY GILBERT TREASURER.

THE slavery agitation in the Mission Boards of our large societies found an origin in a "Communication from a Committee of the Baptist Ministers in and near London, to the Board of the General Convention of the Baptist Denomination for Foreign Missions, on the Subject of Negro Slavery."

This communication was referred by the Board to a committee, consisting of the corresponding secretary and Messrs. Knowles and Stow. In their report, they express their "satisfaction with the spirit of Christian affection, respect, and candor which the communication breathes. They received it as a pleasing omen of a more intimate correspondence and a more endeared fellowship with our Baptist brethren in Great Britain. The committee, however, are unanimously of opinion that as a Board, and as members of the General Convention, associated for the exclusive purpose of sending the gospel to the heathen, and to other benighted men not belonging to our own country, we are precluded by our constitution from taking part in the discussion of the subject proposed in the said communication."

The resolution touching this question reads: "Resolved, — That, while, as they trust, their love of freedom, and their desire for the happiness of all men, are not less strong and sincere than those of the British brethren, they cannot, as a Board, interfere with a subject that is not among the objects for which the Convention and the Board were formed."

The letter was dated September 1, 1834, and in a bold and fearless manner stated in full the peculiar difficulties, which cannot be fully understood by persons in other countries. The letter proceeds to explain the difference between the political organization of the United States and that of England, and this difference makes it impossible to adopt a course similar to that which the British Parliament have adopted in reference to slavery in the West Indies: "This country is not one state with an unrestricted legislature, but a confederacy of states united by a constitution, in which certain powers are granted to the national government, and all other powers are reserved by the states. Among these reserved powers is the regulation of slavery. Congress has no power to interfere with the slaves in the respective states, and an act of Congress to emancipate the slaves in those states would be as wholly null and void as an act of the British Parliament for the same purpose. . . . This view of the case exonerates the nation as such, and the states in which no slaves are found, from the charge of upholding slavery. It is due, moreover, to the republic to remember that slavery was introduced into this country long before the colonies became independent states. The slave-trade was encouraged by the government of Great Britain, and slaves were brought into the colonies against the wishes of the colonists and the repeated acts of some of the colonial legislatures. These acts were negatived by the King of England, and in the Declaration of Independence, as originally drawn by Mr. Jefferson, it was stated, among the grievances which produced the revolution, that the King of England had steadily resisted the efforts of the colonists to prevent the introduction of slaves. Soon after the revolution, several of the states took measures to free themselves from slavery. In 1787, Congress adopted an act, by which it was provided that slavery should never be permitted in any of the states to be formed in the immense territory northwest of the Ohio, in which territory the great states of Ohio, Indiana, and Illinois have since been formed. There are now thirteen states, out of twenty-four, in which slavery may be said to be extinct. Maryland is taking measures to free herself from slavery. Kentucky and Virginia will, it is believed, follow the example. We state these facts to show that the republic did not originate slavery here, and that she has done much to remove it altogether from her bosom. She took measures, earlier than any other country, for the suppression of the slave-trade, and she is now zealously laboring to accomplish the entire extinction of that abominable traffic.

"Since, then, from the character of our political institutions, the emancipation of the slaves is impossible, except with the free consent of the masters, it is necessary to approach them with calm and affectionate arguments." It was claimed that slaveholders were better acquainted with slavery than others; that multitudes were in favor of its extinction, while some "are not convinced that slavery is wrong in principle, just as many good men in England, half a century since, believed the slave-trade to be just and right." The number and character of the two millions of slaves, scattered over a part of the Union, with no large military force to overawe them, and with no provisions to care for the young, the feeble, and the aged, made this subject of emancipation a problem difficult of solution, and, "we presume that the people of England would feel somewhat differently on the subject of emancipation, if the slaves were among themselves, and the perils of this moral volcano were constantly impending over their own heads."

Mention is made of the good feeling existing among the "multiplying thousands of Baptists throughout the land," of their confidence in their love for Christ, of the liberality and zeal characterizing their southern brethren, and of the impossibility of reaching the conclusion that it would be right to use language or adopt measures which might tend to break the ties that unite them to us in our General Convention, and in numerous other benevolent societies, and to array brother against brother, church against church, and association against association, in a contest about slavery.

These reasons induced the Board of Missions to decline an interference with the subject of slavery. "It ought to be discussed at all proper times, and in all suitable modes. We believe that the progress of public opinion in reference to slavery is very rapid, and we are quite sure that it cannot be accelerated by any interference which our southern brethren would regard as an invasion of their political rights, or as an impeachment of their Christian character."

What an advanced scout is to an army, this letter was to the anti-slavery conflict, which began as the sighing of a zephyr, which grew into a tornado that has stranded the navies of our hope, and levelled in the dust the monuments of our pride. The church was offered the front of the conflict. Right or wrong, she judged it to be her duty to hold her opinions on the subject of slavery in abeyance to the paramount interests of the soul. Here was a society engaged in promoting the spread of the gospel throughout the world. Should the Board stop because of a difference of opinion regarding the rights of man? "Christ and his church habitually regarded man as an immortal being; and so absorbing was the thought of his eternal destiny, that they could not stop to discuss the minor questions of the hour." This was the argument. Infidels have denounced both the argument and its advocates; and because ministers and churches have sheltered themselves behind the claims of missions and the requirements of the work, Christianity has been ridiculed. But it should not be overlooked that the reproach heaped upon the church attests its high character and position. Horace Mann won fame as an abolitionist, and as a defender of the rights of human nature. Yet, ten years later, because, forsooth, his little scheme of education was imperilled by the conduct of Rev. S. J. May, in regard to abolitionism, he did not hesitate to write him,* when a single pupil had left the school, "The obvious feeling was, that it was a pity that theoretical anti-slavery should prove to be practical anti-education, by depriving your school of a valuable pupil, and yourself, to some extent, of the respect of an influential citizen." Why did not infidels attack this position? The church lost not only one, but oftentimes hundreds, because of its adherence to the rights of man; and yet because some ministers were silent, rather than promote dissension, there was no language bad enough to express the condemnation felt towards them by the leaders of the abolition movement. The Board of Missions cannot be compared to the Board of Education in Massachusetts, either in the objects it strives to promote, or the cause it endeavors to serve.

Said Mr. Mann, "I confess myself one of those who hold the maxim to be a damnable one, that 'our actions are our own, while the consequences belong to God.' We cannot separate the action from the consequence, and therefore the latter is as much our own as the former." Mr. May, in his reply, claimed that some of the pupils were abolitionists when they came, or were made so by Father Peirce. To this Mr. Mann replies, "Father Peirce had no right to make them so, any more than he had to make them Unitarians, or Bank or anti-Bank in their politics." In time Mr. May is advertised to be one of the lecturers of an abolition course about to be delivered in Boston. About this, Mr. Mann writes, "Every friend of yours, and of the cause with which you hold so important a

* Life of Horace Mann, pp. 169, 170.

connection, is pained beyond measure at this annunciation. Did you not tell me, again and again, that if the public *would let you alone*, in regard to your abolition views, you thought you could get along well enough with your friends? But how can you expect that the public will let you alone, if they find you, every term, making abolition speeches or delivering abolition lectures, and exhibiting yourself as a champion of the cause in a way and on occasions which so many will deem offensive? You must not mistake my motives; and if you think I am speaking too plainly, you must pardon it for the zeal I have in the cause." *

Those who are familiar with the earnest remonstrances of valued Christian friends, when they have felt the interests of souls were imperilled by introducing political questions into the pulpit, will be better able to make apologies for them. The churches did not indorse the position of the Board of Missions. Professor J. D. Knowles, on his return from New York, where he became infected with the disease which hurried him to a premature grave, declared his sorrow that he had ever written this letter of reply to the English Baptists, as it made him appear to be what he was not—the defender of human slavery. This was in 1838. Horace Mann's letters were written in 1843, when the nation was rocking with agitation. It would repay perusal could we present in detail the honorable part the church bore in the anti-slavery reform. The Mission Board was formed in May, 1814, and commenced operations with two missionaries in the field, providentially thrown upon their hands. It is known that Judson and Rice sailed for India as mis-

* Life of Horace Mann, p. 172.

sionaries of the American Board. While on their passage they were converted to Baptist views. They landed upon a foreign shore without money and without friends. When the news reached America it produced a thrill of joy in the Baptist heart. The North and the South joined heart and soul in the work of the Lord. The West was then unknown. The valley of the Ohio and Mississippi was a *terra incognita.* The weakness of the denomination made union imperative. United heart and hand, they had worked together until this letter came from England. The conscience of Christians had been aroused by the efforts made to promote emancipation views in England and in the West Indies.

At this time the war began in earnest. Three years before, William Lloyd Garrison had commenced the publication of the "Liberator" in New England, where he claimed that "prejudices against the negro and freedom were more rampant than in the South."

In 1832 he began to send forth illustrations of the slave-locked in the arms of his wife, being beaten by the overseer; or of the poor slave, kneeling, eyes looking towards heaven, and hands clasped, saying, "Am I not a woman and a sister?" The platform began to resound with appeals; the pulpit sounded a trumpet which gave timely warning; the church prepared for action.

In 1835 a meeting was called in Ritchie Hall, Boston, "to disapprove of all denunciation, personal censure, and severity respecting any of our brethren who may speak or act differently from the wishes of the Board on the subject of anti-slavery." In June, 1835, a letter was sent to the Board disapproving their action in withholding from publication the English letter and the reply.

At this time Rev. William H. Brisbane, who afterwards emancipated his slaves, and became the leading abolitionist of his time, was a pro-slavery editor in Charleston, S. C., and was eager to enter into an argument to prove that slavery was a divine institution, and was sanctioned by the Bible. Then, for the first time, the South began to be pervaded with the thought that the North regarded slavery as a sin against God. Though the Board of Missions owned the "Christian Index," published in Georgia, and was sanctioning slavery in various ways, yet at this time the northern religious press contained very many leading editorials, headed, "The Bible against Slavery."

The policy adopted by the Missionary Board prevailed to a large extent. The "Watchman" closed its columns to the discussion of the question. The "Reflector" was started in Worcester in the year 1838. It was designed to promote the glory of God and good will to man. "Fear God and give glory to him. All Scripture is profitable. God hath made of one blood all nations of men," were the inscriptions written upon this banner of truth.

In a letter written by Rev. Baron Stow to the London Union, January 11, 1839, he says, —

"Among the obstacles in the way of the abolition of slavery, I might name the inhuman prejudice against color as the badge of servitude and debasement; the peculiar organization of our government, reserving to the states the entire control of slavery within our own limits; the opposition of Christians in all the slaveholding states to abolition, and in the free states to all agitation of the subject. It would not be difficult to show that the influence of the American church, at present, is the main pillar of American slavery.

"But, my dear brother, God is on our side, and the cause will prevail. Every day it is gaining friends, and though less rapidly than we could wish, yet steadily and surely advancing towards the desired consummation. Still help us by your prayers and remonstrances, and anticipate with us the joyful day when republican America shall be purified of this foul and deadly leprosy."

On January 6, 1841, the following address was republished at the request of large numbers North and South. The year 1840 gave it birth, but the year 1841 was distinguished by the influence it exerted.

To Southern Baptists.

The American Baptist Anti-Slavery Convention, holding its first session in the city of New York, on the 28th, 29th, and 30th of April, 1840, to the Baptist slaveholders of the Southern States: —

Fathers and Brethren: We have assembled, to the number of one hundred and ten persons, at the written call of seven hundred Baptists from thirteen of the United States. Of this number, about four hundred are accredited ministers of Jesus Christ.

A conviction of duty, which, we humbly conceive, is based upon the fear of God and the love of our fellow-men, — whether bond or free, oppressors or oppressed, — constrains us to submit a few thoughts for your special and candid consideration. In doing so, we appeal, with the firmest confidence, to the Omniscient God for the rectitude of our intentions. We solemnly profess a prayerful and submissive reverence for the principles of his recorded will. We feelingly avow a tender sympathy, not only for the slave, but also for you, upon many of whom slavery is entailed by heritage and enforced by law, while inexorable habits, formed in the passive state of infancy, as well as universal usage, impose bonds upon yourselves scarcely less strong or less oppressive than the fetters of the slave.

Hear us, then, with patience and kindness. It is our firm conviction that the whole system of American slavery, in theory and practice, is a violation of the instincts of nature, a perversion of the first principles of justice, and a positive transgression of the revealed will of God; *for* man instinctively seeks happiness and repels outrage, while slavery compels him to forego the former and endure the latter, for himself and his posterity, until the end of time. Justice, in its very nature, assumes the existence of free moral agents, mutually bound by established principles, and acting towards each other with perfect reciprocity. We do not speak of justice towards a "chattel personal," a horse, or a swine. But the statutes of the South pronounce a slave a "chattel personal to all intents and purposes whatsoever," and thus set him beyond the pale of justice, as utterly disqualified to assert a right and to redress a wrong.

Divine revelation, as committed to Moses and expounded by our Lord, teaches that pious self-love is the only proper measure of our love towards others. Does slavery — especially its laws which quench or smother in the slave the light of the mind, which tear from his agonized bosom the dearest objects of his natural affection — conform to that rule of Holy Writ?

We believe that God only has the right to take away the health, the wife, the children, or the life of men guilty of no social crime. When man, single or associated, uses his power for such ends, he appears to us to arrogate to himself the prerogatives of the Almighty, and to assume a responsibility under which an archangel would stagger.

God, it is true, made use of the Jews to exterminate certain heathen tribes, and to inflict upon others a mild servitude, carefully defined and restricted. To employ this mode of punishment, or any other that he chose, was his unquestionable right. But where is the Scripture warrant to apply this special license of Jehovah for the extirpation of the human race at large, or the enslavement of any nation in particular? This specific direction to his oracular people is but *an exception* that confirms the *general rule* of his Son, "Thou shalt love thy neighbor as thyself."

The heart of the blessed Jesus was, indeed, an overflowing fountain of the tenderest sympathy for human woe. Food, health, and life were his boon, never withheld when solicited; and the gospel preached to the poor was the peculiar and characteristic proof of his being the Son of God and the Saviour of the world.

No evidence exists that he ever witnessed a scene of slavery. It is not shown that Hebrews of that day trafficked in human flesh. The chained coffle, the naked gang of the cotton-field, the exposed female reeking under the lash, the child torn forever from its mother's breaking heart, — these, and worse acts of slavery's tragedy, were not performed, so far as history speaks, before the face of Jesus. But his warmest, almost his only burst of indignation, is against those who devoured the helpless widow's substance, and, for a pretence, made long prayers and liberal contributions to the cause of God.

His itinerant, inspired followers were too busy in draining off the universal deluge of idolatry, explaining the nature of the one living God, and establishing the claims of Jesus as the true Messiah, to define, or to condemn, in form, every species and variety of crime, in every age, that hell, fruitful of inventions, might suggest and fallen human nature perpetrate. Hence, horse-racing, gambling, piracy, the rum traffic, and the African and American slave-trade, remain ungraduated in the Scripture scale of human sins. Paul, however, exhorts the servants of *heathen* masters to respectfulness and patience, for the reason that the name of God be not blasphemed; and advises them, while patient under bondage, to prefer freedom. He enjoins *Christian* masters to give their servants what is just and equal. Do the slaves of American Baptists obtain justice and equity? He implores his brother Philemon to receive again the converted fugitive, not, as he probably had been, the heathen vassal of a heathen lord, but as a beloved brother in Jesus Christ. Thus we behold, in all the Scriptures, a virtual and total condemnation of American slavery.

Besides, American Calvinistic Baptists, as a whole denomination, have been hitherto regarded, by the Christian world, as *responsible for the sins of Baptist slaveholders, and the sufferings of one hundred thousand Baptist slaves.* And if we fail, as many do, to testify our abhorrence of a system that allows a fellow-Christian to sell his brother, or his brother's wife or child, or to dissolve the marriage tie at pleasure, we see not how to escape the merited contempt of mankind, the reproaches of conscience, or the displeasure of God. For the followers of Jesus are ordained the light of the world, and *his witness of the truth* until the end of time.

Further, in the exhaustion of your once teeming soil; the non-increase, and, in some parts, diminution of your white population; the depreciation of your staple products, and the competition of British enterprise in India; the jubilee-shout of West India emancipation, rousing the dormant spirit of your slaves to assert the rights of man; your intrinsic incapacity of self-defence in case of foreign aggression; your constant exposure to servile insurrection and massacre; and in the general reprobation of republican slavery throughout the rest of the civilized and Christian world, — we behold indications that God attests, by earthly signs, the precept of his heavenly oracles, to "let the oppressed go free."

Again: if you have heard us thus far with candor, you may perhaps inquire, "What would you have us do?" We answer, "At once confess before heaven and earth the sinfulness of holding slaves; admit it to be not only a misfortune, but a crime; remonstrate against laws that bind the system on you; petition for the guarantee, to all, of "natural and inalienable rights." If your remonstrance and prayers to man are disregarded, cast yourself on the God of providence and justice; forsake, like Abraham, your fatherland, and carry your children and your households to the vast asylum of our prairies and our wilderness, where our Father in heaven has bidden our mother earth to open her exuberant breast for the nourishment of many sons.

Finally, — if you should (which Heaven avert!) remain deaf to the voice of warning and entreaty; if you still cling to the power-maintained privilege of living on unpaid toil, and of claiming as property the image of God which Jesus bought with precious blood, — we solemnly declare, as we fear the Lord, that we cannot and we dare not recognize you as consistent brethren in Christ; we cannot join in partial, selfish prayers, that the groans of the slave may be unheard; we cannot hear preaching which makes God the author and approver of human misery and vassalage; and we cannot, at the Lord's table, cordially take that as a brother's hand, which plies the scourge on woman's naked flesh, which thrusts a gag into the mouth of man, which rivets fetters on the innocent, and which shuts up the Bible from human eyes. We deplore your condition; we pray for your deliverance; and God forbid that we should ever sin against him by ceasing so to pray.

The war of words now began between the two contending parties. Document met document, and letter met letter. Every newspaper was full of "Our own Views." It had been a period of intense excitement for years. Mob law took the place of civil law, and presses which could not be intimidated by threats, and editors that could not be silenced by argument, were ruthlessly assailed.

On one side stood Elon Galusha, Nathaniel Colver, Timothy Gilbert, and others like them; on the other stood Richard Fuller, J. B. Jeter, and others as fearless and as brave.

In 1841 the effort was made to drop Elon Galusha's name from the Board of Missions. It was successful. Joseph Sturge, of London, commissioned with an address to the President of the United States, signed by Thomas Clarkson, and written "in behalf of the millions of our fellow-citizens held in bondage," on his way from a slave pen, stopped to look in upon the Triennial Convention, and thus, in a letter to a slave-trader writes: "In passing from the premises we looked in upon the Convention of the Baptists of the United States, when in session in the city of Baltimore, where I found slaveholding ministers of high rank in the church, urging successfully the exclusion from the Missionary Board of that society of all those who, in principle and practice, were known to be decided abolitionists; and the results of their efforts satisfied me that the darkest picture of slavery is not to be found in the jail of the slave-trader, but rather in a convention of professed ministers of the gospel of Christ, expelling from the Board of the society, formed to enlighten the heathen of other nations, all who consistently labor for the overthrow of a system which denies a knowledge of the Holy Scriptures to near three millions of heathen at home."

Rev. Elon Galusha, in his letter to Rev. R. Fuller, Beaufort, S. C., had taken the boldest anti-slavery position, and entered into the defence of the slave in a manner so fearless, so kind, so eloquent that it won troops of friends to his cause, and carried dismay to the ranks of the foe. There were hundreds in the Missionary Society that stood by his side. Mr. Sturge overlooked this fact. It was common thus to cast reproach upon the church, and to forget that there were more than seven thousand who never bowed the knee to Baal. The lives of men like Gilbert, Colver, Galusha, and a host of others, prove this. The history of the American Baptist Anti-Slavery Convention proves it. The piles of anti-slavery documents establish the fact. The denominational press proclaims it with trumpet tone.

"You assure us that you are content to appeal to God in justification of slavery," said Mr. Galusha. "You should remember that this whole nation, Christians, ministers and all, once unitedly appealed to God for the truth you deny. They declared that all men are created equal; that they are endowed by their Creator with certain inalienable rights; that among these are life, *liberty*, and the pursuit of happiness. You dwell upon the pleasure of laboring, praying, singing, and communing with fifteen hundred slaves, as though *that* were some part or parcel of slavery, which should commend it to our regard, or which reconciles you to it, or justifies you in supporting it; whereas there is nothing in the genius, the laws, the spirit or tendency of the institution, to produce any such state of things, but entirely the contrary. All which you describe as lovely is to be attributed to humanity and religion, pushing their conquests into the empire of slavery."

This letter abounded in facts. He spread out before the eye the fifteen hundred thousand human beings whom the Presbyterian synod of South Carolina and Georgia, by their committee, say, "will bear a comparison with the heathen in any country in the world." He spoke of their "own missionary (Turpin), who, in giving oral instructions to the slaves, drew forth a remonstrance signed by three hundred and fifty-two individuals, the ground of which was 'knowledge is power,'" and that "intelligence and slavery have no affinity for each other." "You express fears that the church will be rent in twain by this topic. Should it be so, will not the responsibility rest upon those who shall be found to love power more than justice, to love *slavery* more than their brethren whom the monster crushes, and prefer fellowship with that system of human degradation to communion with the church of Christ?" Notwithstanding the opposition of the South, Mr. Galusha is elected president of the Missionary Convention of the State of New York by a triumphant majority, and the feeling is, that there will be a close fight at Baltimore, with a probability of a split of the denomination and a division even among the southern members.

March 24, 1841, the executive committee of the

American Baptist Anti-Slavery Society sends another address to the South, in which slavery is held up as a sin against God, and the violation of every natural right of man. Rejoinders are written, and answers come back. In the spring of 1841, the conflict culminated. The principal benevolent societies of the Baptist denomination met in Baltimore, April 29, and began their work Friday, A. M., April 30. This session was the most important of any in its results. After hearing the treasurer's report, the Convention proceeded to ballot for its Board of Managers. This election included a vote on the name of Elon Galusha. Meetings had been previously held in Baltimore, both public and private, where a ticket had been prepared in which the name of every abolitionist, hitherto on the Board (with the exception of Baron Stow), was left off. In the minutes of the twentieth anniversary of the Georgia Baptist Convention, page 9, there is a reference to the action of this meeting. From this it appears that a meeting of southern delegates was held in Baltimore, on Monday previous to the meeting of the Convention, in which a document signed by a large number of northern brethren was submitted as a voluntary expression of their sentiments. This document determined the southern delegates to take no action till after the election of the Board of Managers. In this election all known abolitionists were left off the Board of Foreign Missions. Baron Stow, a former member of the Board, had been exceptionable at the South; but a letter addressed by him to the Foreign Secretary was read before the meeting of southern delegates, of which a copy was preserved, and of

5*

which the following is the substance: "I do wholly disapprove the denunciatory language so much in vogue with some in regard to slaveholders. I think it not only impolitic and inexpedient, but uncourteous and unchristian. The address of the Baptist Anti-Slavery Convention to southern Baptists I was dissatisfied with at the first reading, and refused to distribute it, as requested, among my friends of the South. I have never been able to satisfy myself, from the New Testament, that I ought to deny any courtesy to a Christian brother because he is a slaveholder." This communication induced the southern delegates to believe it would be impolitic to oppose his reëlection. The election came and passed, and Mr. Galusha's name was dropped. Dr. Fuller, in the convention, declared that he had not been instructed how to vote. It was afterwards proved that he had been instructed by his Association, and had failed to remember or to state the fact.

Dr. Stow had declared himself dissatisfied with the address of the Anti-Slavery Convention. It was afterwards asserted that without objection he had voted to circulate three thousand copies of that address in the South. The letter says, "I refused to distribute it, as requested, among my friends of the South." These facts, spread among the churches, weakened the confidence of brethren in each other, and impaired their influence.

In August, 1841, the Tremont Street church took action, in which the hand of Timothy Gilbert is visible. After reviewing in detail the facts to which we have hastily glanced, they —

"Resolved, 1st,—That the present Board are virtually pledged to the fellowship and support of slavery; that they have willingly given the South so to understand it; that this pledge, as it was intended, has met and satisfied the demands of the South; and that while the studied and peculiar manner of doing it may for a time succeed in blinding the eyes of many to the character of the operation, it is in reality none the less a departure from the appropriate work of the Convention, nor any the less effectual in prostituting the moral influence of that organization to the support of slavery, than if it had been done in a more frank and official manner.

"Resolved, 2d,—That, connected as were the doings of the Convention at Baltimore with the above defined compromise document in the rejection of brother Galusha and others from the Board, and also with the intimation given at the time by brother Fuller, that it was to prevent the South from withholding their funds, we cannot divest the transaction of the appearance of bribery; and that the Convention has assumed to itself a position of dictatorship over the disciplinary operations of the churches at once dangerous to their independence, their peace, and their purity; and that so long as it maintains its present position, while our interest in the cause of missions is unabated, we are constrained, as we regard the cause of truth and righteousness, the responsibility of the churches to Christ, and the cause of missions itself (which has been put in jeopardy by their transactions), to seek some other channel through which our contributions may flow to the heathen, until these afflictive obstructions are removed out of the way."

Thus was sounded the note of alarm, and ground was broken for the organization of the provisional Committee. This was a period of intense excitement. In the North, as in the South, men took the position, that however right it may be to condemn slavery by vote in a meeting of citizens, it is a sin to condemn it by vote in a convention of Christians. "My kingdom is not of this world" — "Render therefore unto Cæsar the things that are Cæsar's" — were texts ever on the world's broad tongue.

There was another side to the picture. In Hamilton, N. Y., August 17, 1841, the American Baptist Anti-Slavery Convention, in a meeting composed of two hundred and eight prominent Baptists, declared, —

1. That the system of American slavery, by regarding immortal men, not as sentient beings, but as things or chattels personal in the hands of their owners, is subversive of all human rights, and a sin against God, who hath made of one blood all nations of men.

2. That immediate repentance of the sin of slavery is the duty of the master, and immediate emancipation, under the protection of law, the right of the slave.

3. That for us to extend the hand of church fellowship to those who continue to practise, or in any way justify, the system of American slavery after due gospel labor, is virtually to bid them God speed, and thus to become partakers of their evil deeds.

4. That to acknowledge slavery to be a great evil and sin, and yet to put forth no efforts for its overthrow, and especially to continue our unrestrained fellowship with those who practise it, is palpably inconsistent with the obligations of the disciples of Him who was manifested to destroy the works of the devil.

This Convention, composed of men who were true to the slave, among whom were Jacob Knapp, Elon Galusha, John Blain, Lewis Raymond, J. L. Hodge, Cyrus P. Grosvenor, took ground in favor of adhering to the Triennial Convention; but "if any cannot conscientiously contribute their funds through the general treasury, we recommend them to commit such free-will offerings to the executive committee of the American Baptist Anti-Slavery Convention through their treasurer, Simon G. Shipley, Esq., of Boston." They declared that the American Colonization Society's enterprise not only passes by the slave, but degrades the free negro, while it opens its arms to receive the lowest class of white emigrants from foreign nations, and elevates them to a participation in all the privileges of our institutions.

Bold and uncompromising as were the positions taken, they failed to satisfy the time-honored abolitionists of Massachusetts. Among that number was Mr. Gilbert. He did not believe in temporizing. From the first he took the most ultra position, and refused to countenance slavery in any way or form. In his subscriptions to benevolent societies, he made specifications that the money given should not be used to aid in the extension of slavery, and if possible that it should be used to eradicate the evil.

In April, 1842, Rev. Nathaniel Colver publicly took his stand in favor of a separate missionary organization. Money began to flow in for the support of missions, without its going through the hands of the Board. In the American Baptist Anti-Slavery Convention, held in Boston, May 18, 1842, Rev. Elon

Galusha in the chair, the following resolution passed unanimously: —

Resolved, — "That at the commencement of the session, this afternoon, special prayer be offered to God for wisdom to direct."

In compliance with the resolve, prayers were offered by several brethren in succession, which were characterized by deep tenderness and solemnity. The crisis had been reached, and the plan of the provisional foreign committee was adopted, which, after setting forth the grievances of those, who, "while they believed it to be the duty of all who enjoy the privileges of the gospel of Christ to use their best endeavors to furnish them to those who are enshrouded in the darkness of heathenism, — the genius of the gospel itself being that of a missionary enterprise, intended to enlighten and recover a lost world, — yet felt that the connection of the foreign missionary operations with slavery was grossly inconsistent with the principles of the gospel, resolved to open a new channel of communication with the heathen, and with our missionaries already in the field, through which we may fulfil our obligation without compromising principle or weakening our testimony against the sin of slavery."

Now that the society was ready for business, Timothy Gilbert stepped to the front, and was elected treasurer, and at once set about opening a correspondence with the heathen world.

The conflict now raged all along the lines. The provisional committee was denounced, and it was applauded. Good men refused to sustain it, and good men came to its aid. In the front of this battle of words was Nathaniel Colver. Charge upon him from what side they chose, he was alike invulnerable. The church now met in Tremont Chapel, under the Boston Museum. They numbered nearly four hundred members, and were pronounced "a devoted and efficient body of Christians."

The decks were cleared for action. The wants of the world abroad united with the wants of the world at home in driving God's honored columns to seek help from on high. This period of consecration, and of devotion to the cause of the slave, preceded a period of blessing such as the church has seldom been permitted to enjoy. The fountain was made full at home, that the stream of benevolence might flow forth to make glad the waste places of earth.

CHAPTER VII.

MR. GILBERT'S LETTER-BOOK. — REFLECTIONS CONCERNING THE DUTY OF CHRISTIAN MEN AND CHURCHES TO THE SLAVE ABSORB HIS THOUGHTS, AND FLAME OUT FROM HIS CORRESPONDENCE. — THE PROVISIONAL COMMITTEE AT WORK. — CORRESPONDENCE WITH MISSIONARIES AND OTHERS. — DRS. FULLER AND WAYLAND ON SLAVERY. — DR. HAGUE'S REVIEW.

In January, 1841, Mr. Gilbert commenced preserving his more important letters. They reveal an extended and comprehensive system of benevolence, a love for the slave that never falters, and a watchful eye over the interests of his Master's cause.

In these letters the condition of the denomination is mirrored. In January, 1840, he writes, "Men and women here, as a general thing, seem to be attending to everything but the one thing needful, the conversion of the soul. The wise and foolish virgins slumber together. We are looking and praying for a visit from the Saviour with the influences of the Holy Spirit. At times we have felt that he was at the door. A few mercy drops have fallen, but when we look at the desolations of Zion here, and in other parts of the country, we feel the need of divine help."

To Rev. Jacob Weston, Jamaica, he sends a box,

with cheering tidings concerning the spread of anti-slavery views, and gives an account of a discussion in the Kentucky Legislature.

To a missionary just starting he gives excellent advice concerning the privations to be encountered and the work to be performed, and asks him to "consider that these trials are but for a moment, while they promise to work out for you an exceeding and eternal weight of glory." Later he writes, "The cause of emancipation in the country is onward, as the signs of the times indicate, although most of the churches, both North and South, are on the side of the oppressor. If you have seen the doings of the last Triennial Convention, held at Baltimore, as reported by all except those opposed to abolition, you will see that the Board, in their individual capacity, have taken sides in favor of the slaveholders, and against the abolitionists, and have called our refusal to commune with slaveholders 'a new test of Christian fellowship.' But the Lord reigns, and has brought, and is bringing, their counsels to nought, and will, no doubt, carry forward his cause by it, and thus make the wrath of man to praise him." August 11, 1841, because of the exclusion of the claims of the dumb and suffering slave from the columns of the "Watchman," with regret he withdraws his countenance and support. December 9, 1841, he writes Rev. C. P. Grosvenor, that there is a feeling in the minds of many brethren that another man would be less objectionable as the editor of the "Reflector." On reflection he fears he may have injured his feelings, and writes him a letter full of assurances of sympathy and of appreciation, and adds, "Yet I am compelled to admit that, with many, your name is objectionable." As a result, his name is dropped, and, in 1842, the paper appears without a nominal editor, but under the supervision of Simon G. Shipley, J. W. Parker, and Clement Drew. January 29, 1842, he writes his brother, "We are in the 'midst of a gracious revival. The Lord is pouring out his spirit and converting sinners. Many have, as we hope, passed from death unto life, and many more are pressing into the kingdom. Elder Knapp is laboring here, and his labors have been much blessed. Although he has been opposed by the enemies of God, yet the opposition has been overruled for God's glory, and the work progresses. Although you are away from it, yet you are as near the Saviour in your lonely dwelling as we are in Boston; and if you offer him the *humble* and contrite heart, he will just as readily own and dwell with you there as here." February 17, 1842, he writes John Sartain relative to the engraving of Jacob Knapp, and makes arrangement to have it finished in the highest style of art. Letters now follow to a relative, chiding him for negligence and sloth; to a friend in England, inquiring about the character of a guest in his house, who came a stranger in the name of a disciple; to dear brother John W. Wilson in Georgia, who wants to borrow money, and who finds great trouble in getting on in the South. August 13, 1842, he withdraws from the committee of the Massachusetts Abolition Society, for want of time to attend to its duties, but continues his support. September 14, 1842, he opens an account with Baring, Brother, & Co., London, and sends one hundred pounds to Rev. Adoniram

Judson, as treasurer of the provisional committee, with the following letter: —

"Rev. Adoniram Judson. Dear Brother: The provisional foreign mission committee of the American Baptist Anti-Slavery Convention have voted to appropriate five hundred dollars, to be forwarded to you, to be expended by yourself and brother Wade in Burmah, for the mission cause. In case you should not sympathize with our conscientious views, you will consult with brethren Wade and Kincaid, and if either or both enter into our views, so far as to prefer to receive their support in whole or in part from us, they may rely upon our remitting immediately and regularly the requisite amount. We do not wish those who shall elect to be thus supported, to separate themselves from the old Board, unless they prefer it, but are willing they should maintain their old relations, report through that channel, while they acknowledge the receipt of funds from the committee. This arrangement is designed to continue so long as that Board shall maintain its present ground in favor of slavery.

Permit me to say, that nearly all of the abolitionists are hearty friends of the cause of missions abroad and at home; but while they help the heathen in India, they are not willing to forget three millions of oppressed heathen in America, who are forbidden access to the Word of God, and who cannot be taught to read the Bible except severe penalties are incurred by the person thus guilty of instructing them. And this wickedness is sustained by professing Christians and by Baptists. Will not God be avenged on such a relation as this? We beg you to view this subject in the light of truth and righteousness, remembering that heathen at home are being sold by professed Christians to obtain money to send the gospel to heathen abroad."

In October he writes again, and forwards documents: "We hope you will candidly review this record of the doings of the Triennial Convention at Baltimore, and the action of our committee, and let your testimony go forth to the churches in this country in favor of the heathen here, as well as the heathen in India. Surely if there is any class of men in the world, of whom it can be said they have no helper, it is the slave in our own country. Husbands are separated from wives, children are torn from parents, and yet a system legalizing these atrocities is justified by ministers and churches who profess the religion of our Lord Jesus Christ. O that God would influence his servants in far distant lands to lift up a *wail* in behalf of those whose cry has been stifled and shut out because of the power of their oppressors, which has controlled the Mission Board, and made them willing to suppress this cry, lest the slaveholder should not give his money and sustain their operations, as though money could convert the heathen, while God has said, 'I hate robbery for a sacrifice'! We do not wish injury to the perpetrators of those deeds, but we ask that they may repent their folly before they meet these crushed ones at the bar of Jehovah. We believe that a proper testimony from the missionaries would do much towards setting the churches and the ministers, and through them the nation, right, and leading our rulers to establish justice and righteousness in the land."

On November 9, there appeared in the "Reflector" a letter from Rev. D. L. Brayton, missionary at Mergui, British Burmah, which indorsed the position of the Baptist Anti-Slavery Society, and used this language: "The *awful* fact that the Bible is kept from the slave, is a consideration which has always most deeply affected my heart. . . . Another thing I have thought much of, is, the inconsistency of those who say, 'We are as much opposed to slavery as you are.' These brethren acknowledge slavery to be a sin. Now, the Bible expressly says, 'Suffer not sin to rest upon a brother.' The Bible commands, 'Search the Scriptures;' slavery prohibits it. My wife and self observe the monthly concert for slaves, and feel deeply to sympathize with you in all your opposition and toil in this great and good work. We are happy to know of your success thus far, and trust that the time is not far distant when the rights of man shall be universally acknowledged, felt, and acted out by his fellow-man." In the same paper, Timothy Gilbert appears in print: "A brother from Hartford informs us that one of the authorized agents of the old Board stated that the five hundred dollars voted to them by the provisional committee had not been paid over, and suggested the query, whether the committee had the funds; and if so, why not pay them over, as the income was small, and the expense of agencies was great? In answer to which, he, and all others who desire to know the facts, are informed, that the committee never voted either five hundred dollars, or any other sum, to the old Board, but voted that five hundred dollars be sent to the Rev. Messrs. Judson and Wade; and they have just received advices from the mercantile house in London through which the money was sent, that it has been forwarded by the overland mail to Mr. Judson. The committee have seven hundred dollars on hand, and will, no doubt, soon have missionaries of their own in the field, unless the old Board retract their testimony which they have given in favor of slavery, and against those who were trying to purify the churches from it, so that we can again coöperate together." December 7, letters from Mrs. D. B. S. Wade and Mrs. Sarah Judson fanned the flame which was spreading throughout the North. "It seems to us," said Mrs. Wade, "passing strange that any person having a true missionary spirit should not, of course, be an abolitionist. Can you suggest any plan for benefiting those now groaning in bondage? There is one subject which has pressed heavily upon my heart, and I have found relief only by carrying it, as I do the wrongs of my poor brethren in bonds, to the throne of grace, and that is the unkind and unchristian spirit often manifested by abolitionists. And I fear that this has grieved away the Spirit and presence of God from many of those who have advocated a cause precious in his sight. This I fear more than all the apologists of slavery can do, for all our hope for the poor slave is in God. It is true we are to have no 'fellowship with the unfruitful works of darkness, but rather reprove them;' but, then, what compassion, what gentleness, what forbearance, what kindness, does the situation of our poor slaveholding brethren require from us? Ought we not to feel for them, even as Christ did, when he wept over Jerusalem?"

"Though we live in a dark, heathen land," said Mrs. Judson, "where our ears are daily assailed, and our hearts constantly pained, by exhibitions of moral wretchedness, yet this cannot drown the loud and bitter cry of slavery, as it is borne to us, from time to time, over the wide ocean, from the distant shores of our beloved, though guilty country. The friends of emancipation are engaged in a fearful contest, but it is a contest of light with darkness, of justice with oppression, and the final victory is, therefore, certain. A system so contrary to the spirit of our blessed Saviour, so fraught with violence and oppression to man, for whom he died, must inevitably give way, as the influence of that heavenly spirit becomes more and more prevalent."

In the same number we find a denial, from the hand of Baron Stow, of "pledged neutrality," saying, "I never authorized any person or persons to give any pledge in my behalf, or to create any 'understanding' in any mind with respect to my future course; and I have yet to learn how 'the southern delegation' were led to consider me as 'pledged' to 'neutrality,' or as in any sense engaged 'to have nothing more to do with Anti-Slavery Conventions.'" The tide was rising.

Returning to the letter-book, we find, January 10, 1843, a letter in regard to Rev. Jacob Knapp's contemplated visit to Washington, "to attack the stronghold of the devil in another form from the one in which you are engaged. I trust, if he is successful, it will be an entering wedge, which will, with the one you are driving, help rend asunder the bonds of slavery. As Mr. Knapp is an avowed abolitionist, and, among other sins, does not fail to expose slavery, I hope you will do all you can to strengthen his hands while among those who may, I fear, thirst for his blood; and if it is not too great a favor, please keep me informed of the progress of the work."

May 11, 1843, Mr. G. writes Rev. J. Wade, Tavoy, Burmah, in which he communicates the fact, that "the Female Missionary Society of the Tremont Street church sends a bell, weighing one hundred and fifty pounds, to be used on his chapel in Burmah; documents of American Baptist Anti-Slavery Society; and the information that the committee have seventeen hundred dollars, which they will use to establish some new mission disconnected with slaveholders, or for the support of some of the missionaries now in the field, should any of them signify a wish to receive support from such a source. The majority of the abolitionists have not so much objection to receive the money of slaveholders, as to be associated with them in evangelizing the world, and thus, by the copartnership, acknowledge them to be Christians in good standing in the Baptist church, instead of bearing our testimony against them, and complying with the injunction, 'Come out from amongst them, and be ye separate.' 'Have no fellowship with the unfruitful works of darkness, but rather reprove them.' Should the whole Christian church bear their united testimony against slavery, as against every other sin, I believe it would soon wither under the rebuke; but so long as there are slaveholders in the southern portion of our country, and those who justify and apologize for it in other sections, connected with and fellowshiped by the church of our Lord Jesus Christ, where shall we look for the salt to purify the fountain from this awful pollution, if it is not found in the church of Christ?" In a letter to Rev. L. Ingalls, same date, he says, "The abolitionists think that slaveholders should not be regarded as members in good standing in the Baptist church, and thus object to any connection that shall be considered as indorsing their Christian character."

In April, 1843, the Baptist Board of Foreign Missions held its anniversary in Albany. A resolution passed unanimously, without discussion and with very little remark, which, it was hoped, would afford relief and gratification to many anxious minds. For the first time the subject of slavery is introduced into the report of the doings of the Board. "Whereas it appears to have been extensively understood, that by certain transactions at Baltimore, during the last session of the Convention, the neutral attitude of the Board, in relation to slavery, was changed, therefore, Resolved, — That the circular issued by the Acting Board, in the year 1840, asserting 'their neutrality on all subjects not immediately connected with the great work to which they are especially appointed,' be reissued and printed with the report of this year, as expressive of the sentiments and position of the Board." In that circular, the positions were taken, that the "exclusive object of the founders of the General Convention, as expressed in the preamble to the constitution, was to send the glad tidings of salvation to the heathen, and to nations destitute of pure gospel light;" that the fathers were careful to lay no obstructions in the way of any individual contributing to its funds; that by the constitution the right to a seat or representation in the Convention is based on two conditions: First, that the religious body, or the individual, be of the Baptist denomination; and, second, that the same shall have contributed to the treasury of the Convention a specified annual sum; and that in regard to the continuance of Christian fellowship between northern and southern churches, it does not come under their cognizance in any form, nor within scope of the Convention with its present constitution. "The churches are independent communities; they can exercise no authority over one another; they have delegated no power to individuals or associations, within the knowledge of the Board, to act for them." In reply to the circular of the provisional committee, Rev. Solomon Peck, D. D., corresponding secretary, used this language: "The neutrality of the Board has not been yielded either at Baltimore or elsewhere. During the whole of our proceedings, since the first agitation of the subject of slavery, it has been our earnest endeavor, as it was our *avowed policy*, to mind *exclusively* the missionary duties to which we had been called."

On May 3, 1843, the American Baptist Anti-Slavery Convention, among other resolves, hastened to declare the action of the Board of Missions satisfactory, and "provided for the continuance of the provisional committee for the purpose of making a proper appropriation of missionary funds now on hand, and to receive such future donations as would not otherwise be made by those who cannot conscientiously contribute to the support of missions through the channel of the present Board." As a result, a new organization, known as the American and Foreign Missionary Society, was formed. Mr. Gilbert did not unite with it for reasons which were to him satisfactory. "When I shall become convinced," he writes to the "Reflector," "that there is no good reason to hope that the old missionary organization will purge itself from the charge of receiving money in such a way as to enter into a copartnership with slaveholders, and giving its sanction to that wicked institution, then I shall be prepared to abandon them, not provisionally, but forever." August 9, 1843, a letter from Dr. Judson was published, in which he acknowledges the money, and speaks encouragingly of the prospect of Mr. Chandler and others acceding to the terms proposed. In a note, published August 23, 1843, after regretting the unadvised publication of Dr. Judson's letter, he expresses the wish, "that the missionaries and the anti-slavery brethren at home should not anticipate the result of the next meeting of the Triennial Convention, but continue to pray, that after that meeting, no obstacle may continue to prevent the cooperation of all the enemies of oppression in the missionary enterprise."

Turning now to the letter-book, we are prepared to understand the statements made in a note, dated September 27, 1843, and addressed to Rev. J. Wade. "If you have written the old Board of your determination, you will, no doubt, before you receive this, or by the same conveyance, have received a letter from them, stating that our committee is dead; or perhaps they may say the difficulty is all settled. That you may have a true statement of the facts, I will endeavor to give them to you in brief. At the meeting held in Albany the Board reaffirmed their neutrality, and reprinted the circular of 1840. As the maintenance of neutrality was all the majority of the abolitionists required, they have done little besides reiterating their understanding of the position taken by the Board, and the character of the compromise made.

"A portion of the abolitionists determined to wait another year before forming a new missionary organization, contenting themselves with the provisional committee, which was formed to meet an emergency, but expected to end in a permanent organization, unless the Triennial Convention should by an unmistakable vote obliterate the record which gave sanction to the sin of slavery.

"A portion of the abolitionists thinking otherwise, have formed a new missionary organization, to be forever separated from the sin of slavery. I did not enter the new organization, preferring to wait so long as there is the least ground for hope that the difficulties may be settled. In the mean time the provisional committee will disburse funds which may be intrusted to them.

"We feel that God requires of us to seek to purify the churches of this awful sin, believing that the power of the church is essential to its eradication from the world. You ask, 'Do professing Christians keep their slaves in ignorance of the gospel?' They most assuredly do. The laws of every slave state make it a great offence to teach a slave to read. Notwithstanding this, some are taught to read in secret by those who commiserate their condition, and have the moral courage to do right — say perhaps one in a hundred; the remainder are excluded from all knowledge of the letter of the gospel.

"Your views in relation to receiving money from slaveholders correspond with my own. I am perfectly willing to receive funds, but would not solicit them for missions from a distiller, a rum-seller, or a slaveholder. Nor would I receive them, if by so doing I should lead him to think that I fellowshipped his sin. If I faithfully expose and rebuke his sin in violating the law of God, then, if after this he should offer me money for the heathen, I should receive it; but at the same time I should tell him that nothing but repentance towards God, and faith in Jesus Christ, could in any measure remove the guilt of his transgression. It is not because the old Board has received the money of slaveholders that we object to their course, but because with the reception of the money there has been a tacit admission of the Christian character of the slaveholder, seen in his being placed upon the Board, and in his being welcomed as a brother beloved in the Lord. Against this the abolitionists protested. For this they were left off from the Board, and the brand of public condemnation was affixed to the name of Elon Galusha." In conclusion he informs the missionary that nothing he may write to the old Board on this subject is permitted to find its way to the public through the press, or is accessible to us who may wish to learn your views."

In the "Reflector" of October 11, 1843, the note of triumph was sounded, and the intelligence is communicated to the public that Rev. J. Wade, of Tavoy, has thrown himself upon the provisional committee for support, desiring to be sustained separate from the unpaid toils of the slave. "This to me is a matter of joy and thanksgiving, inasmuch as slavery must be driven from the church before it can be driven from the world; and I trust that this decision of brother Wade will ultimately do more to take away from slavery the shield that the churches of our denomination have thrown around it, than any one act, besides, since the commencement of the anti-slavery feeling in the land. A meeting of the provisional committee was held, and Rev. Duncan Dunbar led in prayer. It was voted to adopt Rev. J. Wade as missionary, and make arrangements for remittance of funds, while the letter of acceptance in which the missionary stated the reasons for his action, was sent to the 'Reflector' for publication." In this letter proof has been furnished that God, by his Spirit, worked upon the hearts of his servants in mission lands, leading them to take a decided stand against the foul system of slavery, which had nearly crushed our missionary operations by its deadly embrace, while the few devoted followers of Christ were taking a decided stand in opposition to the on-rushing tide of evil. His words bore the ring of the warrior and the burning glow of a Christian's zeal. "How slaveholders can give their money to send the gospel to the distant heathen, and yet approve of a policy which keeps their slaves in ignorance of the same gospel, is to me a paradox. Slavery, as it exists in America, is, I consider, a monstrous evil, both to the master and to the slave; an outrage upon justice, a disgrace to the American flag, and the reverse of all Christian principles. I cannot suppose that it will survive the first dawnings of the millennial age. I need not advert to Mrs. Wade's views on this subject. It is enough to say she is a member of a female anti-slavery society, and will of course be gratified to know that no part of our support is to be derived from the unpaid toil of the slave."

"The committee pledges itself to sustain any missionary who prefers to receive his support in whole or in part, rather than be a partaker of the contributions of slaveholders. *This I prefer.* I suppose the committee means to be understood as saying it will give the same support that the Board now gives, and that what are termed extra expenses will be paid by it as they now are by the Board. With these provisos I cheerfully accept the pledge, — not that I feel so conscientious about receiving support from slaveholders that I would sooner give up my work and leave the heathen to die ignorant of the gospel than receive such support, for I think, though slaveholders will not do justice to their slaves, yet the Lord has claims upon them relative to his cause among the heathen; but so far as receiving such support goes to strengthen slavery, I wish to discard it."

In regard to the condition of affairs, Mr. W. writes, "I felt persuaded there was some cause, besides the hardness of the times, for the reduction of that mighty stream, which, a few years ago, was pouring into the treasury, to so diminutive a rill as at present. Why should missionaries be recalled, schools, and other means for evangelizing the heathen which have been prosperously commenced, be abandoned for want of funds, while nothing is wanting to supply them but a proper channel through which they may flow without doing violence to the conscience? The doings of the committee have anticipated the very thing which I proposed to brother Kincaid to attempt, if he should see cause for it."

Thus, it appears, the provisional committee met a felt want of the denomination, and kept open the channels of benevolence in regions where the sins of a pro-slavery church had served to quench the flowing forth of the stream from the fountains of loving and believing hearts.

In a letter dated October 14, 1843, Mr. Gilbert addresses the following cheering words to the uncompromising missionary: "The committee rejoice in the opportunity to sustain a missionary who will join with us in bearing his testimony against one of the crying sins of the nation. You may rely upon it, that your conduct will thrill with joy the hearts of those who have sighed and cried over the abominations that are done in the land; and we doubt not but it will be, with the blessing of God, an important means in bringing the churches to the decision that slaveholding is inconsistent with good Christian character. You need have no fear but that you will be amply sustained by those who feel opposed to the American system of slavery.

"We wish you to understand distinctly that the old

Board has studiously withheld from publication everything you have written on this subject. They do not hesitate, in many instances, to misrepresent us and our motives, by claiming that we desire to break up established order in society. True, there are abolitionists who have acted with us, as well as many who have been connected with the churches, that have gone off in favor of woman's rights, no government, &c., &c., but those who act with the provisional committee, as well as the great body of the abolitionists connected with our organization, are church-going and church-supporting people, who believe and sustain the distinguishing doctrines of the Bible and of the Reformation, and are hearty supporters of those who preach Christ and him crucified as the only hope of the sinner, and that without any compromise with Unitarianism or Universalism. While this is true of Christian abolitionists, it may be said to be a characteristic of the pro-slavery portion of the church that they wish to let alone the popular sins of the day, when opposing them exposes to public censure. For myself, — and I may say the same thing of my brethren, — we acknowledge no masters in the flesh, and deem it our first duty to inquire as to the will of God: if, with the best light we can obtain, we feel that he will commend, we go forward, feeling that, while duty is ours, consequences belong to God. This, I think, should be the course pursued by all who love our Lord Jesus Christ. This spirit must animate the missionaries abroad, or their labors will be barren of results; for, no doubt, the policy that makes the pro-slavery church dumb in the presence of the Moloch of slavery, would tempt the missionary to try and win the favor of the heathen by compromising truth, in hope thereby of getting their good will, so that by and by they might gain greater influence over them. We hope, however, that you will never attempt any such compromise, but will unflinchingly do the Lord's will. We may add that your past course gives the most unequivocal assurances of your conduct for the future."

"As to your relations with the old Board, I will say that there is very little probability that they will allow you to receive your support from us, and yet be considered their missionary. I fear they will discard you altogether for this act, unless they entertain a hope of your retracting in future. All we ask them to do, is to withdraw their shield from the slaveholders, and no longer defend or vindicate their Christian character while they cling to that sin; but this they refuse to do. They condemn our action, and stand as a barrier between us and the slaveholders. I write this with pain, yet fidelity to you makes a plain statement of the case a duty. But let us rejoice because of the presence of the Lord in our midst, and of the providences which are fast driving slavery from its hiding-place in the church of Christ. We have much to encourage us in the signs of the times in this country; and I verily believe that those who cleave to that abomination will soon be crushed with it, as those were among the Philistines when Samson bowed his head and bore away the pillars of the temple. I pray God that he may cause his people to come out from among the defenders of slavery, and thus purge his church. It is the desire of the committee that harmony may characterize the councils and labors of the missionary, and that there may be no strife because of the spirit of dissension born of the discussion of slavery at home. Be Jesus Christ's men. Let there be no other strife than to see who shall be most like his Master in devotion to the interests of humanity, and in bearing an uncompromising testimony against sin."

At this time the "Watchman" accused Deacon Gilbert of inconsistency, because he was willing to receive the money of slaveholders in exchange for merchandise. In reply, he says, "I consider money or produce, whether by the unpaid toil of the slave or in any other way, articles that may be rightly received for pianos or any other goods, without inquiring as to the source from whence they come. Those articles are neither better nor worse for passing through my hands or the hands of a slaveholder; otherwise we must go out of the world for money, to get that which we could be sure had never been paid for unrighteous uses. It is not the money, but the price paid for it, which makes it corrupt in the hands of the holder, whether that price be a fellow-man or his unpaid labors, or *barely* the extending our Christian fellowship, as is the case with those who now receive the slaveholder's money for missions; for I presume it will not be denied that the withdrawal of such fellowship would as effectually exclude their money as a direct refusal to receive it; the first we are bound to do for the benefit of the slaveholder as well as the slave, but the last I think we have no right to do. Although slaveholders may buy my goods, they cannot, either directly or indirectly, buy my intentional sanction to the system of American slavery; and if, with the knowledge of this fact, they withdraw from me their patronage, I am prepared to forego that; but if, with this testimony against wickedness, they wish to purchase my goods, I have no scruples about receiving their money, as I give them a fair equivalent; and once in my hands it is the same as if received from any other person, although in their hands it might have been corrupted because of the unrighteous manner in which it was obtained; but now that they have exchanged it for goods that were mine, those become the corrupted articles, and so does every thing he may buy with it. See Deuteronomy xxviii. 15–21. I further would say that my influence, and whatever income God may give me, either from the patronage of slaveholders or any other source, shall, according to my best judgment, be made to bear upon that wickedness until it is driven from the church of Christ, and from all our social or political institutions; and this I hope to do without reference to the sneers or frowns of slaveholders or their apologists, either at the North or South. If the American Board of Foreign Missions will publish their condemnation of slavery as unequivocally as this, and consistently carry it out by withdrawing all Christian fellowship from slaveholders, then there will no longer be cause for continuing the provisional committee, or any other organization disconnected with that Board; but we can all unite in the support of missions, and I doubt not but every friend of the oppressed in our denomination cherishes the same view."

Mr. Gilbert's correspondence now reveals the deepening hold of the claims of his Master's cause. He mourns over the desolations of Zion, and bewails the worldliness creeping into the church, and fears that "policy so intermingles with piety, that God cannot bless his people without exalting their pride."

"A stream never rises higher than its fountain, and it is to be feared that the cause of Christ in heathen lands will suffer from the low state of piety here."

"A leading man in one of our churches recently advocated building and finishing churches in such style as to draw in the rich, in order that we may obtain their money to aid in the diffusion of the gospel. But to me this did not possess the characteristics of Christ's plan or preaching, who declared, 'The poor have the gospel preached to them.'" Mr. G. explains his view in regard to free-seated houses of worship, in private memoranda, in letters, in speeches, and conversation. In writing to a missionary in the autumn of 1843, he says, "This building churches for the rich excludes the poor. They are not included in the plan. If they attend church, they are not welcomed to the body of the house, but are sent to the pew for the poor, or to the gallery. This serves to banish them from the house of God. The little church with which I am connected is on the free-seat plan. Here the rich and poor can meet together; and the black and white are entitled to the same privileges. The Lord has so far prospered us that we have purchased the late Tremont Theatre, and expect soon to have it ready for use. It will seat about twenty one hundred persons, and it is in the heart of the city, convenient and accessible to all, cost fifty-five thousand dollars, and will require about twenty-five thousand dollars to fit it up, but, when complete, will have connected with it stores and other rooms for rent, the revenue from which, we expect, will meet the interest of the debt. The church, because of its anti-slavery character, has very little sympathy or assistance from the wealthier portion of our Zion; but God has almost miraculously helped us, and our prospects brighten as the months speed on."

November 16, 1843, he writes Mr. Wade, and gives him needed information in regard to the character of the assistants about to sail for India. "I would remark that there are two missionaries and their wives, and a Miss Lathrop, who is intended to assist Mrs. Wade, about to sail. The latter has been prevented from seeing me, and I have sought in vain for an interview. The Missionary Board seem unwilling that any one identified with the provisional committee should converse with her. They fear our influence. *I shall see her if possible.* One of the men is a Mr. Binney, who has been a pastor of a slaveholding church in Savannah, Georgia, and in a conversation, where I was present, about two or three years since, proved himself to be a bitter opposer of the abolition movement, and was what I should call one of the most violent of pro-slavery men. If he has altered in his views it is unknown to me. We consider that the object of the Board in sending him out is to propitiate the feeling of the slaveholders, in order to get them to contribute for the support of missions; but to us, that seems to be paying an unwarrantable price for aid. Unless they can assure the South that they fellowship slaveholders as Christians, they cannot obtain funds in that quarter; and if they do thus assure them, they provoke the divine displeasure, and divorce themselves from the sympathy and support of the haters of slavery in the North." Mr. G. regrets that the Board persists in clinging to the South. "We presume they expect Mr. Binney to disabuse your mind of any unfavorable impression you may have received concerning the slaveholders. They utterly refuse to publish anything from the missionaries which can offend the South. Is it strange that God frowns upon such conduct?"

The following letter from Mr. Wade lays bare to the eye the heart of this apostle to the Karens. It is written to Rev. Solomon Peck, D. D., corresponding secretary of the Board of Missions: —

TAVOY, April 23, 1844.

DEAR BROTHER PECK: On the 20th of last month I had the pleasure of receiving your letter to me in answer to the one I wrote you requesting permission of the Board to accept the offer of the provisional committee to provide for my personal support from their funds. In your answer you say, "The acceptance of your personal support from the provisional foreign missionary committee, retaining also your connection with the Board, is an arrangement to which the Board cannot accede."

Permit me to ask why the Board cannot accede to it. Has the Board adopted it as a *general rule* not to accede to the proposition of any society, church, or individual, to support a missionary through the medium of the Board, despite the wish of such missionary to receive his support in that way? I suppose not; and believing that the Board has some *particular* reasons in this case why they cannot accede to such an arrangement, I shall, therefore, waive this subject. The Board have said they cannot accede to such an arrangement in this case. This answer is *decisive*. In a letter to Mr. Gilbert, dated January 29, 1844, I did accept the offer of support from the provisional committee, they having acceded to the terms which I submitted to them in a letter dated January 27, 1843. Here, I think, the matter must rest until I learn the results of the Triennial Convention, which meets this month. The first remittance of the committee — one hundred pounds — I have credited to the Board, and have drawn on the Board for my salary and extra expenses up to the 1st of January, 1844, which I trust the Board will approve.

Having now been informed that the Board cannot accede to the arrangement of my drawing *personal* support from the committee, yet being under the direction of the Board, I shall open accounts with the committee from the 1st of January, 1844, hoping and praying that the results of the meeting of the Triennial Convention will be such that myself and all the abolition Baptists can *conscientiously* resume our former relations with the Board. At present the reasons which induced me to accept personal support from the committee remain. . . . You say, "The receipt of support or aid, from whatever source, has no necessary connection with slavery; and still less ought it to be wrested into an approval or sanction of slavery." I admit it; the connection is not a *necessary* one. As I said in my first letter to the committee, slaveholding brethren have a duty to perform in sending the gospel to the heathen, from which injustice to the slave does not excuse them. They ought to aid in the support of missions; and missionaries receiving support from them do not thereby, under *ordinary* circumstances, involve themselves in the sin of slaveholding. If a man offers me money for the support of missions, I shall not ask him whether he is a slaveholder, a distiller, a Catholic, a Mussulman, or a Christian, taking it for granted, that, whoever he be, he does well in wishing to promote the missionary cause; whoever he be, it is right for him to put his money into the treasury of the Lord, "for the earth is the Lord's, and the fulness thereof." But if he intimate that his offering is a kind of oblation to the idol of slavery, the demon of intemperance, the beast, or the false prophet, and that, in taking it, I must bow to his idol, or, at least, I must agree not to denounce it, and, so far as my influence extends, not tolerate any one who does denounce it, — I would then reject it, for his sake that showed it, and for conscience' sake, "for the earth is the Lord's, and the fulness thereof." When slaveholders make the exclusion of abolitionists from the offices of the Board the *condition* on which they aid the missionary cause, I cannot, *conscientiously*, receive support from them on *this condition*. Let the condition be withdrawn, let Mr. Galusha be restored to his office in the Board, let the question of slavery and anti-slavery have no influence on the doings of the Convention, or in the obtaining of funds, and I shall no longer have any scruples about receiving my support as formerly. It is the condition on which slaveholding brethren pay their money which constitutes my objections to receiving it.

The expulsion of Mr. Galusha from his office in the Board was not, I admit, an act of the Board, as a Board. No; it was the act of the Convention, and I now want to see if the Convention will not, at its present meeting, adopt measures which will heal the breach made by those of their last meeting. That they may do so, is my earnest prayer.

We have with great pleasure heard of the arrival of the new missionaries at Maulmain, and are now daily anticipating the still greater pleasure of welcoming them to Tavoy.

I remain, dear brother,

Very affectionately yours,

(Signed) J. Wade.

In the letters which follow Mr. G. expresses his pleasure at the reception of letters which prove that missionaries abroad keep step with the church at home in the holy crusade against slavery. He speaks of the dedication of the Tremont Temple December 7, 1843, of the capacity of the house, of the crowds of young men and women which are gathered to listen to the searching discourses of his pastor. Sketches of sermons are often sent, texts are quoted, and the leading thought is set forth. February 27, 1845, he refers to a paper written by Rev. D. Sharp, D. D., in reply to resolutions forwarded by the Alabama State Convention, asking whether a slaveholder could receive an appointment as a missionary. The No is emphatic and decisive, and the manliness of the reply will tell upon the conflict now raging. It reads as follows: —

BOSTON, December 17, 1844.

DEAR SIR: We have received from you a copy of a preamble and resolutions which were passed by the Baptist State Convention of Alabama. As there is a demand for distinct and explicit answers from our Board to the inquiries and propositions which you have been pleased to make, we have given to them our deliberate and candid attention. Before proceeding to answer them, allow us to express our profound regret that they were addressed to us. They were not necessary. We have never, as a Board, either done or omitted to do anything which requires the explanation and avowals that your resolutions "demand." They also place us in the new and trying position of being compelled to answer hypothetical questions, and to discuss principles, or of seeming to be evasive and timid, and not daring to give you the information and satisfaction which you desire. If, therefore, in answering with entire frankness your inquiries and demands, we should express opinions which may be unsatisfactory or displeasing to you, our plea must be, that a necessity was laid upon us. We had no other alternative, without being wanting, apparently, in that manly openness which ought to characterize the correspondence of Christian brethren.

In your first resolution, you say, "that when one party to a voluntary compact between Christian brethren is not willing to acknowledge the entire social equality with the other as to all the privileges and benefits of the union, nor even to refrain from impeachment and annoyance, united efforts between such parties, even in the sacred cause of Christian benevolence, cease to be agreeable, useful, or proper." In these sentiments we entirely coincide. As a Board, we have the high consciousness, that it has always been our aim to act in accordance therewith. We have never called in question your social equality as to all the privileges and benefits of the Foreign Missionary Union. Nor have we ever employed our official influence in impeaching or annoying you. Should we ever do this, "our united efforts," as you justly say, would "cease to be agreeable, useful, or proper."

In your second resolution, you "demand the distinct and explicit avowal, that slaveholders are eligible and entitled to all the privileges and immunities of their several unions, and especially to receive any agency, mission, or other appointment which may fall within the scope of their operations and duties."

We need not say that slaveholders, as well as non-slaveholders, are unquestionably entitled to all the privileges and immunities which the constitution of the Baptist General Convention permits and grants to its members. We would not deprive either of any of the immunities of the mutual contract. In regard, however, to any agency, mission, or other appointment, no slaveholder or non-slaveholder, however large his subscriptions to foreign missions, or those of the church with which he is connected, is on that account entitled to be appointed to an agency or a mission. The appointing power, for wise and good reasons, has been confided to the "Acting Board," they holding themselves accountable to the Convention for the discreet and faithful discharge of this trust.

Should you say, "The above remarks are not sufficiently explicit; we wish distinctly to know whether the Board would, or would not, appoint a slaveholder as a missionary,"—before directly replying, we would say, that in the thirty years in which the Board has existed, no slaveholder, to our knowledge, has applied to be a missionary. And, as we send out no domestics or servants, such an event as a missionary taking slaves with him, were it morally right, could not, in accordance with all our past arrangements, or present plans, possibly occur. If, however, any one should offer himself as a missionary, having slaves, and should insist on retaining them as his property, we could not appoint him. One thing is certain: we can never be a party to any arrangement which would imply approbation of slavery.

In your third resolution, you say, that "whenever the competency or fitness of an individual to receive an appointment is under discussion, if any question arises affecting his morals, or his standing in fellowship as a Christian, such question should not be disposed of, to the grief of the party, without ultimate appeal to the particular church of which such an individual is a member, as being the only body on earth authorized by the Scriptures, or competent, to consider and decide this class of cases."

In regard to our Board, there is no point on which

we are more unanimously agreed than that of the independence of churches. We disclaim all and every pretension to interfere with the discipline of any church. We disfellowship no one. Nevertheless, were a person to offer himself as a candidate for missionary service, although commended by his church as in good standing, we should feel it our duty to open our eyes on any facts to the disadvantage of his moral and religious character which should come under our observation. And while we should not feel that it was our province to excommunicate or discipline a candidate of doubtful character, yet we should be unworthy of our trust, if we did not, although he were a member of a church, reject his application. It is for the Board to determine on the prudential, moral, religious, and theological fitness of each one who offers himself as a missionary; it is for the church, of which such a one is a member, to decide whether he be a fit person to belong to their body.

The other resolutions, which were passed in your recent Convention, regard more your own action than ours. They therefore call for no remarks from us. We should have been gratified, in the present impoverished and embarrassed state of our treasury, if the brethren in Alabama, confiding in the integrity and discretion of the "Acting Board," could unhesitatingly have transmitted to us their funds. We have sent out missionaries and enlarged our operations, in the expectation that, so long as we acted in conformity with the rules and spirit under which we were appointed, we should be sustained both by the East and the West, the North and the South. If in this just expectation we are to be disappointed, we shall experience unutterable regret.

We have, with all frankness, but with entire kindness and respect, defined our position. If our brethren in Alabama, with this exposition of our principles and feelings, can coöperate with us, we shall be happy to receive their aid. If they cannot, painful to us as will be their withdrawal, yet we shall submit to it, as neither sought nor caused by us.

There are sentiments avowed in this communication, which, although held temperately and kindly, and with all due esteem and Christian regard for the brethren addressed, are, nevertheless, dearer to us than any pecuniary aid whatever.

We remain, yours truly,
In behalf of the Board,
DANIEL SHARP, *President.*
BARON STOW, *Rec. Sec.*

REV. JESSE HARTWELL,
President Alabama Baptist State Convention.

The effect of this document was apparent in the North and in the South. Virginia Baptists, in full Convention, instructed the treasurer of their State Convention to pay over no more money. Other states took similar action. The meeting of the Triennial Convention, to be held in Providence, began to be looked forward to with overwhelming interest, inasmuch as an attempt would be made to reverse the decision of the Board. The provisional committee took action on the subject, and unanimously approved the decision of the Board, and in the last of March, 1845, issued the following address: —

Address of the Provisional Committee.

At this crisis in our missionary operations, the Provisional Foreign Mission Committee deem themselves called upon to publish the following distinct expression of their views and feelings. The committee was organized with reluctance, to meet an exigency believed *then* to exist. It was honestly supposed that previous transactions had committed the Baptist Board of Foreign Missions to the support of the institution of slavery, so as to render further coöperation with them a connivance at that sin. It never has been our desire that the Convention, or its Board, should turn aside from their appropriate work, to contend against slavery; all we wished was, that they would oppose it and its claims, when, like idolatry, or licentiousness, or intemperance, it should seek to resist, or impede, or corrupt the great enterprise of spreading the gospel in its power and purity. Yet it was painfully observed that slaveholders were too successfully endeavoring to subordinate this organization to their aid, in opposing the free action of northern brethren and churches against their favored institution. They sought to compel their coadjutors here by threats of displeasure, and a disruption in case of a refusal, to publish to the world, either individually or officially, directly or indirectly, that slaveholding does not disqualify any one for church membership, or for the ministry, or for the office and work of a missionary, and that it is no sin. And their supposed success at Baltimore, in 1840, prevented them *then* from withholding their funds and withdrawing from the Convention.

Doubtless many of our brethren were deceived respecting the design of those transactions, and were thus made to contribute to results which they did not anticipate. But if at *that time* the real intention of slaveholders to subject the missionary organization to the interests of their cherished system was not detected, their *recent* attempt has been less successful. Their threats of disunion, withholding funds, &c., so often made to constrain the Board to abandon their appropriate duties, and give countenance to slaveholding, have now met with a merited rebuke. In their last movements their aim has been sufficiently obvious to convince even the most wavering of the character of their former designs. But through the ordering of Providence, and the fidelity of the Acting Board to their convictions of duty, the South have obtained so much testimony against their "peculiar institution," as will leave them hereafter in no doubt respecting the estimation in which slaveholding by the ministry is held at the North. Thus they have constrained the Board to do all that we ever desired. And we are happy in believing and declaring, that they have thus removed all cause of suspicions of any connivance with, or responsibility for, the sin of slavery. Should the South continue to contribute to the Board after what has been said, we should regard such funds as those received from irreligious men, the reception of which does not involve the Board in the guilt of the donor. So long as they maintain this position with that candor and firmness with which it has been taken, we feel free to say, that we shall give them our *most cordial support*, and we believe it is the solemn duty of all who love the cause of missions, to come to their aid with that devotion and liberality which its present languishing condition demands. . . .

All who prefer openness and candor to concealment and intrigue, cannot fail to honor the Board for the manner in which they have answered the questions lately put to them by a portion of the South. No doubt the latter would like to reverse the decision; but they, as well as we, desired that a decision should be made. From the necessity of the case, an answer must be fatal to the hopes of one or the other party, and prevent their continued harmonious coöperation. But an evasion of the difficulty would have been more so. The character and spirit of slavery, and the light pervading Christendom, in our judgment, render a decision inevitable. If the entire North sustain the Board, the line will be drawn, where it belongs, between freedom and slavery. And indeed, wherever the line may run, it will separate between those who uphold slavery and those who refuse to do so.

To such as have felt constrained, with us, to withdraw their direct cooperation with the Board for a season, we say with deep sincerity and emotion, *See to it that our brethren are sustained in the honorable stand which they have taken*, and which, we doubt not, they will maintain. For us *now* to stand aloof would be base and treacherous. Gratitude to God for an event for which we have earnestly prayed, should keep us from such a course. So much of the support of the cause as has hitherto come from the unpaid toils of the slave, will, no doubt, now be withheld; let this deficiency be more than made up by your increased liberality. Let not the Board and the missionaries suffer, because the former refuse in any way to sanction a system of wrong which has been alike grievous to us all. The missionaries in Burmah once had it under consideration to request the Board to deduct from their scanty salaries the probable amount secured from slave labor, and it was not that they would not have deemed privation a luxury, compared with the thought that the means of their own support were in part the price of some Christian brother or sister sold into perpetual bondage, — a doom more dreadful than death, — that this resolution was not taken.

Let this fact, and others still more plainly indicating the harmony of their views and feelings with our own, impel us to exert our utmost to afford hearts so noble all they desire for their own comfort, and for the success of that cause which we all so much love. We entreat you to allow no partiality for contention, and no vain excuse, to deter you from giving immediate and convincing evidence of your sincere and firm attachment to this holy enterprise. Let us remember those who consecrated their all to it, and bear in mind that we are no less the Lord's. Let those whose funds have been conveyed through another channel now promptly direct them to this. And if for any cause any have kept back their donations, let them see to it that they are now honestly paid over to the treasury of Him who will not be robbed with impunity.

By order and in behalf of the Committee,

S. G. Shipley, *Chairman.*

Geo. W. Bosworth, *Secretary.*

In the midst of increasing excitements the meetings in May came on. The action of the Convention was mild, temperate, and firm. The committee, of which Dr. Wayland was chairman, to whom the Alabama resolutions were referred, reported that,

All members of the Baptist denomination in good standing, whether at the North or South, are constitutionally eligible to all appointments emanating either from the Convention or Board.

While this is the case, it is probable that contingencies may arise in which the carrying out of this principle might create the necessity of making appointments by which the brethren at the North would either in fact, or in the opinion of the Christian community, become responsible for institutions which they could not, with a good conscience, sanction.

Were such a case to occur, we would not desire our brethren to violate their convictions of duty by making such appointments, but should consider it incumbent on them to refer the case to the Convention for its decision.

All which is respectfully submitted, in behalf of the committee.

F. WAYLAND, *Chairman.*

Rev. Dr. Welch opposed the reception of the report, on the ground that it is too ambiguous to meet the expectations of the denomination in this period of earnest agitation. He remarked that we are called as honest Christian men to meet the question, whether the North and South shall coöperate in the great work of foreign missions. He proposed to add to the report resolutions sympathizing with the Acting Board in their trying circumstances, and fully sustaining their late actions.

The third article was then adopted.

Rev. Dr. Welch's resolutions were again read.

The first, which was ultimately adopted, was as follows: —

"Resolved, — That we sincerely and deeply sympathize with our brethren of the Acting Board, charged with the interests of the missions during the recess of the Convention, in the responsibilities they sustain and the difficulties with which they are surrounded, and we now pledge to them our cordial coöperation and liberal support."

The second having been again read, Rev. Mr. Jeter arose, and stated that the South would never have participated in forming the Convention, if they had not supposed themselves on terms of perfect equality with their brethren at the North. He thought it, therefore, not improper for the Alabama Baptists to address the Board as they did. They had, besides, some special reasons. The Board, he remarked, "were bound to reply; and their reply he understood as at first, notwithstanding all explanations. It made slaveholding a disqualification. And as doing so it cuts off the South from all participation in managing the affairs of the Board. We regard the position of the Board as unconstitutional. If they had left us an inch to stand upon, we would have remained in coöperation with the Board. But, said he, we have not that inch left. We are cut off. He wished the brethren of the

North union among themselves, and feelingly adverted to his own position as a slaveholder by necessity, rather than by choice."

Rev. Dr. Williams dissented from the second resolution of Dr. Welch. It seemed to him that the adoption of the resolution would destroy the unity of the report of the committee. He thought the report, as it stood, adapted to produce a soothing effect — a soothing effect at the South, though coöperation cannot be maintained — a soothing effect at the North, which would tend to harmony in this section of the Union. He desired the separation to be relieved of its unhappy features, and to be marked by such sentiments of piety and affection as should be approved by the Holy Ghost. He thought we had done well to pass the first resolution, expressing our sympathy with the Board, but thought it could do no good to go further.

Rev. Dr. Stow was opposed to the passing of this resolution. "First, it would tend unnecessarily to exasperate the South. The South are about to withdraw — let us not, said he, give bitterness to the separation. Second, there are many in the Northern and Middle States who do not sustain the Board, and these he would not exasperate. And, third, the Acting Board do not desire it; the first resolution is all that they desire. If the Board pledge their sympathy, and continue their coöperation, no more is desired. The doings of the Acting Board are before the world, and may be left to stand or fall upon their own merits."

On May 7, 1845, the American Baptist Anti-Slavery Convention held its last anniversary in the McDougal Street Baptist Church, New York.

Satisfied with the action of the Convention, and convinced that their organization had been fully vindicated, and that the purposes which called it into existence had been won, it was voted "to dissolve the provisional committee, and that the executive committee be instructed immediately to pay out all funds in their treasury for the support of Mr. and Mrs. Wade, or, in case of their death, that the committee pay out these funds for the support of other Baptist anti-slavery missionaries, and that the treasurer be directed to receive no more funds for the purpose of either domestic or foreign missions; that the necessity which called into existence this Convention is met, or may be met, more fully by other anti-slavery organizations or movements; that the executive committee carry into effect the resolution for the disposal of the funds as soon as possible, and then publish that fact, and announce the dissolution of the American Baptist Anti-Slavery Convention."

Thus were brought to a triumphant close the doings of a body whose influence was felt in foreign climes, and whose noble and persistent bearing in favor of gospel and political freedom changed the character of our great organizations, and laid bare, to the gaze of mankind, the impiety, the tyranny, and the monstrosity of American slavery. At this point Mr. Gilbert separated from many of his co-laborers; they adhering to the fortunes of the American and Foreign Baptist Missionary Society, while he gave his unqualified support to the Missionary Union from that time on to the close of his eventful life.

Though a triumph had been won in the North, the

principles touching slavery held by men of prominence were sadly at variance with his own. The correspondence, as printed in the "Reflector," between Drs. Fuller and Wayland excited surprise. He felt a contempt for the effort made to prove that Christianity sanctions slavery. When Dr. Fuller declared, "I find my Bible condemning the abuses of slavery, but permitting the system itself," he claimed that he was disgraced as a Baptist. In his estimation, the concessions of Dr. Wayland, that "the New Testament contains no precept prohibitory of slavery," yielded up the ground, and permitted the southern champion to bear off the palm. In 1846 William Hague, D. D., read before the Conference of Baptist Ministers a review of the discussion, which found its way into print in the year following, and has become memorable, because it met the argument of Dr. Fuller by the maintenance of positions which covered the point that Dr. Wayland had left vulnerable.* The article has a noteworthy history. It evidenced that too much had been conceded to pro-slavery writers. Dr. Thompson and Dr. Cheever, who examined its positions, corroborated every one of them, and acknowledged their indebtedness to the review; while Theodore Parker spoke of it as being a contribution of permanent worth to the cause of human freedom. In it the position is affirmed that apostolic Christianity actually abolished slavery, the relation of owner and chattel, whenever

* It is entitled "Christianity and Slavery," and may be found in the excellent volume which has been issued by Gould and Lincoln under the title of "Christianity and Statesmanship."

both of the parties acknowledged the supremacy of the law of Christ, as members of a Christian church.

Those acquainted with Mr. Gilbert's peculiar views can imagine how he would relish this mode of handling the professed advocate of the slave. We quote from the review: "The mode in which the new dispensation is supposed to have borne upon the slave system is thus expressed by Dr. Wayland: 'By teaching the master his own accountability; by instilling into his mind the mild and humanizing truths of Christianity; by showing him the folly of sensuality and luxury, and the happiness derived from industry and frugality and benevolence, it would prepare him, of his own accord, to liberate his slave, and to use all his influence towards the abolition of those laws by which slavery was maintained. By teaching the slave his value and his responsibility as a man, and subjecting his passions and appetites to the laws of Christianity, and thus raising him to his true rank as an intellectual and moral being, it would prepare him for the freedom to which he was entitled, and render the liberty which it conferred, a blessing to him as well as to the state, of which he now for the first time formed a part.'"

This Deacon Gilbert rightly thought conceded too much, and so he gave his assent to the utterance that the statement, as made by Dr. Wayland, "falls far short of the truth, and grants a great deal too much." "It is yielding to the advocate of slavery an advantage which in Dr. Fuller's hands has been made to take on the aspect of a triumph." "All the world confess that Dr. Wayland is an elegant writer and a strong reasoner; but the strongest reasoner cannot *create* truth; the highest result that he can achieve, in a discussion like this, is to use effectively the elements of truth and power with which reason and revelation have furnished him. But, after such a concession as this, we cannot conceive it to be within the scope of the human intellect to impart to the scriptural argument against slavery an appearance of great strength. To give it force and poignancy, to direct it with quickening and commanding energy to the conscience of the slaveholder, are "impossible." Dr. Hague then showed that the Epistles of Paul containing the passages referred to were addressed, not to the world at large, nor to the subjects of the Roman empire as such, nor to men as men and citizens, but to little communities of Christians, who had come out from the world, and had risen above the level of Roman law to a higher moral realm wherein Christ swayed a sceptre of sovereignty; unto whom, looking up, they could say with the voice of common adoration, in response to his own announcement to them, Thou alone art our Master, and *all we are brethren.* He showed that slavery had been for centuries abolished among the Jews, and that the right of slave property under Roman law did not inhere any more in the relation of master and servant than it did in that of parent and child. Then taking up the Scripture references, he showed that all harmonized with the apostolic declaration, "God hath made of one blood all nations of men to dwell upon all the face of the earth;" and that "for disciples of Christ there was no need of instructions to inform them that one of their number had no right to hold the other as property." In other words, he showed that, as the element of chattelship, of absolute property, inhered, as a fundamental principle of Roman law, in the relation of the wife to the husband and of the child to the parent, as well as in that of master and servant, if Christianity impliedly sanctioned slavery, or chattelship in the servile relation, it was equally sanctioned, by parity of reasoning, in the conjugal and filial relations. Every wife was a slave to the husband, every child was a slave to the father, in accordance with Christianity. The argument of Dr. Fuller proved too much, and, of course, proved nothing. The following declaration gave expression to Dr. Hague's thought, and in a clear manner defined the position of the disputants: "The man who, in the view of the civil law, is regarded as a slaveholder, but who, in heart, abhors the system, testifies against it as unrighteous, and does what he can to bring it to an end, is guiltless compared with him, either at the South or North, who never owned a slave, but who says that Christianity sanctions slavery. The one is the unwilling victim of the system; the other is the voluntary advocate of a principle which, if true, fixes on Christianity all the guilt of the system itself. The one exerts an influence which tends to destroy the system, the other an influence which tends to perpetuate it. The one utters a testimony, however feeble, in harmony with the voice of the Bible; the other muffles God's trumpet, so that it can pour forth no note of warning, but only gentle sounds, which soothe rather than alarm the conscience of the oppressor."

This review comforted Timothy Gilbert, and made him a fast friend of its author. He welcomed a defender of the Scriptures from the ranks of his own denomination with greater pleasure, because men of distinction had in his estimation disgraced themselves, and done lasting injury to the cause of truth by furnishing infidels weapons by which they might with a promise of success assail the citadel of truth. This argument of Dr. Hague has remained uncontroverted, because it is uncontrovertible. It enables men who are not scholars to be true to the oppressed without being false to their faith in the gospel of Christ, and proves Christianity fit to win its way through all tribes of men, as a universal religion. It shows that the Messiah of ancient prophecy, who was to be the Deliverer of the oppressed and the Desire of all nations, the Preacher of liberty to the captive, has come and established his kingdom on the earth.

CHAPTER VIII.

DEDICATION OF TREMONT TEMPLE. — THE DEATH OF MRS. GILBERT. — SECOND MARRIAGE OF MR. GILBERT. — TRIP TO EUROPE. — CONSECRATION OF HIS PROPERTY TO THE CAUSE OF CHRIST.

THE dedication of Tremont Temple to the service of Almighty God was an event of special significance in the life of Timothy Gilbert. On June 26, 1843, he received the deed of Tremont Theatre, and put the same on record. Though he had wrought manfully in the anti-slavery cause, and, as we have seen, had carried on an extensive correspondence with missionaries, statesmen, and ministers, yet, could we have seen the under-currents of his life, we should have found that the one great object to which he had consecrated himself, was the erection of a free place of public worship in the heart of Boston. He believed that such a building would exert a telling influence upon the history of all large cities, and help to stay the incoming wave of infidelity and Romanism. His tactics were worthy of a Grant. He determined to hold the centre of the line, believing that all would then be well. The crowded condition of the Baptist churches, the thousands of strangers and mechanics wandering in the streets, and uninvited and unwelcomed to the courts of the Lord's house, touched his heart and made him resolute in his purpose.

The prejudice against the negro, the vital necessities of the poor and neglected, caused him to plan the erection of a building whose rental should defray expenses, and furnish in a hall, without cost to the church, accommodations for a multitude sufficiently large to make the support of a minister a burden so light that it might easily be borne by the poorest.

He went into an estimate as to the amount which would be required from each individual, and published a card showing the results of one, two, three, and four pennies, contributed each week by the stated worshippers. Impressed with the feasibility of the project, he purchased Tremont Theatre for some sixty thousand dollars, opened it for the service of Almighty God, and invited Rev. Lyman Beecher, D. D., to preach the first sermon before the theatre was changed, and then made it ready for the uses of worship. The work was completed, and the building was dedicated on Thursday evening, December 7, 1843. A severe snow-storm that had prevailed during the day, and which continued with much violence in the evening, induced the fear that few would be present. Those who are unacquainted with the anxiety felt by the burden-bearers of an enterprise of this magnitude, can hardly appreciate their solicitude in such an hour.

Deacon Gilbert's faith shone forth conspicuously on such occasions. He did his whole duty, and then trusted to God for a blessing. On this occasion, as on many others, his faith met its sure reward. Over fifteen hundred persons were present at the opening of the meeting. The services were commenced with a voluntary on the organ and anthem. The Rev. Mr. Caldicott offered the invocation. Scriptures were read by Rev. John O. Choules, when the following hymn, written for the occasion by the pastor, Rev. Mr. Colver, was sung: —

Great God, before thy reverend name,
Within these ransomed walls, we bow;
Too long abused to sin and shame,
To thee we consecrate them now.

Satan has here held empire long, —
A blighting curse, a cruel reign, —
By mimic scenes, and mirth, and song,
Alluring souls to endless pain.

Fiction no more! God's truth, at last,
Shall here portray eternal scenes;
The gospel peal the battle blast,
Or charm with Calvary's gentler strains.

Here set thy feet, O Zion's King,
And send thy victories all abroad;
Blest Dove, distil from balmy wing
The dew of life — the grace of God.

Thus let the glorious war go on,
The banner of the cross unfurled;
Soon the last triumph shall be won,
And Christ possess a ransomed world.

Sermon, by the pastor, from John xii. 31, 32. Anthem. Dedicatory prayer, by Rev. William Hague, D. D. The second hymn was written by H. S. Washburn, Esq.: —

O Thou who canst create anew,
And change the dross to purest gold,
This house — which once its votaries drew
To scenes of vice, when vice grew bold —

Accept as thine, Jehovah, King,
  New-formed and fashioned for thy praise;
And overshadow with thy wing
  The altar that to thee we raise.

And long may youth and hoary age —
  Come up to worship in thy fear,
And hand, and heart, and voice engage
  To bless the God of Jacob here.

O God supreme, thy power maintain,
  And turn the hearts of men to thee;
Till He whose right it is shall reign,
  Lord of the heavens, the earth, the sea.

After which, the service was concluded with the benediction, by Rev. Rollin H. Neale, D. D.

The "Daily Mail," in noticing it, says, "Mr. Colver carries a very brier in his hand, and sinners must look out or they will be touched in tender places. He is no time-server. He preaches for eternity. There is no half work about the worthy pastor; he cries aloud and spares not. His sermon was founded on the proposition that the cross of Christ is both the pledge and the instrumentality for the defeat of Satan's plans and the overthrow of his kingdom. It was concluded by a series of reflections and an argument in favor of houses of worship with *free seats*." "Here, within these walls, men of all ranks, conditions, and complexions, are on an equality. The rich, the polite, the fashionable, are welcomed, but only on condition that the poor man, meanly attired, may occupy the seat beside them. All, without distinction, are invited to come up hither, listen to God's truth faithfully dispensed, and worship before high Heaven."

The old building differed in many respects from the one now occupied by the church. The lecture-room measured eighty-eight by ninety feet. It contained two hundred and eighty pews, measuring three thousand feet in length, and would seat over two thousand persons. But its galleries projected badly over the audience, and it lacked the symmetry and elegant proportions that go to make the hall of the present Temple the finest auditorium of its size in the world. The chapels in the old building were not as extensive nor as convenient as are the present rooms of the Meionion and Vestry. But the edifice was an arrow-shot ahead of anything then in existence in the United States. It was declared to be an ornament to the city, and the hope was expressed that it might prove of immense advantage to the cause of truth and righteousness. "The public and the Tremont Street church," so says the "Reflector," "are indebted chiefly to the enterprise and liberality of Deacon Timothy Gilbert, for the speedy and successful accomplishment of this noble work. Others have done what they were able, but on no man has the burden rested so heavily, and by no one could it have been borne more cheerfully than it has been by him. We congratulate him and his coadjutors on what God has enabled them to do, and commend the church, with its pastor, to the blessing of Him who must build the house, or they labor in vain who build it."

It is seldom the day of adversity is set so closely over against the day of prosperity, as was the case on this occasion. While every heart was jubilant with joy, and flooded with the radiance of hope, a cloud was gathering over the sky of him who had climbed to his Pisgah and had seen his Canaan. His wife, devotedly pious, was accustomed to share with her husband in his trials and labors and sacrifices for the cause of Christ, not as though they burdened, but as though they blessed her. She had entered with delight into the work of building Tremont Temple, and without a murmur saw her private fortune imperilled for the public good. The snow-storm, though it did not deprive the Temple of an audience, was the cause of her sickness and sudden death. The carriage in which she rode to church was given to one, who, in her opinion, needed it more than herself, while she walked home through the snow; and that night, while her husband was asleep, the shadow from the wing of the death-angel fell upon the partner of his life.

Her moan awaked him. Leaping up and striking a light, he found her suffering from paralysis. Everything that medical skill could devise was tried, but in vain. In one brief week Timothy Gilbert followed to the grave the joy of his heart and the light of his eyes, at the age of forty-seven years and five months. The papers of the time bear abundant testimony to her worth. "We might," said a friend in the "Reflector," "write a long eulogy upon her character and life: her quiet, unobtrusive, ever-useful way of living makes her pathway to heaven luminous." The number of ministers, missionaries, and of men, who, as youth, were made welcome to her table, and made happy by her society, attests her hospitality, generosity, and worth.

Among the number is Hon. H. S. Washburn, who wrote this brief tribute to her character, which was sung at her funeral, December 16, 1843: —

Calmly to thy grave we bear thee;
  Sainted mother, take thy rest!
Tears will flow, but trust in Jesus
  Shall assuage the wounded breast.

Widows mourn that thou hast fallen,
  Orphans shed the bitter tear,
And the House of Zion weepeth:
  Who is not a mourner here?

Quickly from us did thy spirit
  Unto glory pass away;
But as twilight shadows linger,
  Will thy blest example stay.

Calmly to thy grave we bear thee;
  Soft will be thy lowly bed;
Tears will flow, but drops of gladness
  Mingle with the tears we shed.

On February 1, 1844, there appears in the "Reflector" this beautiful expression of the high regard which another entertained for her character: —

Kindness all her looks expressed;
  Charity was every word;
Her the eye beheld and blessed,
  And the ear rejoiced that heard.

Wealth with free, unsparing hand,
  To the poorest child of need,
This she threw around the land,
  Like the sower's precious seed.

Oft her silent spirit went,
  Like an angel from the throne,
On benign commissions bent,
  In the fear of God alone.

Then the widow's heart would sing,
  As her home with comfort smiled,
And the bliss of hope would spring,
  On the outcast orphan child.

Help to all she did dispense —
  Gold, instruction, raiment, food,
Like the gifts of Providence,
  To the evil and the good.

Deeds of mercy, deeds unknown,
  Shall eternity record,
Which she durst not call her own,
  For she did them to the Lord.

Sudden, yet prepared, she died;
  And, victorious in the race,
Won the crown for which she vied,
  Not of merit, but of grace.

Among the letters of condolence received are two or three that deserve notice. On January 2, 1844, Rev. Jacob Knapp wrote Mr. G. from Wilmington, Del., "We felt very sensibly the shock when we opened your letter and read the sentence, 'My dear wife is dead.' But, as you say, your loss is her gain. I know not that I ever found the person in all my travels who was more crucified to the world, more entirely consecrated to God, more constantly and ardently breathing out that spirit of benevolence and good will to man which the gospel inspires, than your dear departed companion; and you and many others have reason to be thankful that God had spared her to you so long, that she was permitted to see your only child brought up and converted before she was taken from you. We shall never forget her kindness to us. She was all that an own mother could be to my wife, children, and myself; and beyond all doubt she is now reaping her reward. The time is short that remains for us to work. Soon you will all meet again before the throne of God, for I believe you can say it is well with me, it is well with my wife, it is well with the child."

The following letter was received by Mr. Gilbert from his early pastor. It shows that though they were walking in separate paths, yet the bonds of sympathy remained unbroken: —

BOSTON, December 15, 1843.

AFFLICTED FRIEND: I most sincerely sympathize with you in your irreparable loss. May the Father of spirits support you under this sudden and very affecting bereavement. I knew your dear Mary, now no more, from the time she was quite a young woman; and I do say, with truth, but with a melancholy pleasure, that amid all the changes and fluctuations of life, I have never for a moment ceased to love and respect her for her many most excellent traits of character.

She was, in my view, distinguished for good sense, great candor and kindness, a thoughtful consideration of the poor, and a consistent Christian piety. She will be a loss to the community, and a loss to the church, of which she was an active and worthy member, — and O, what a loss to you and your daughter!

Well! Be still, and know that He who hath permitted this sad event is God.

I shall leave the city to-morrow, or I would have attended the funeral as a token of my sincere sympathy for you and regard for her memory.

Yours truly,

DANIEL SHARP.

MR. TIMOTHY GILBERT.

But Mr. G. could not pause long at the grave. The current of life swept him on, and the cause of Christ demanded his energies and his time. He did not get along well without a home. His daughter was at this time away at school, and he felt alone. In the course of time he became acquainted with Miss Alice Davis, a member of the First Baptist Church, who became his wife November 28, 1844. In this choice he felt, and had cause to feel, that the Spirit of God guided him. She made his home as happy as a home could well be. In prosperity, as in adversity, she shared his thoughts, heard what he wrote, knew his plans, watched his moods, and gave him in her heart a refuge from the storms that beset his path.

In writing to her, he reveals his indebtedness to his first wife, his anxiety for the church, and his hope that her influence and watchcare may stimulate him to the better discharge of his Christian duties.

In 1846 they adopted Alice, born April 23, 1846, and in the following year, April 27, Martha Fear Gilbert was born. The heartiest of welcomes was given to this last birdling. In 1851 Mr. Gilbert and wife found relaxation in a trip to Europe, which afforded enjoyment and rest. During his absence Mr. G. wrote letters to the church, to his pastor, and to his workmen, describing the scenes best calculated to interest them.

Nathaniel Ripley Cobb, who was born near Portland, November 3, 1798, and who died on the 22d of May, 1834, exerted a powerful influence upon the life and fortunes of Mr. Gilbert. Mr. Cobb was one year younger than his friend, had been baptized one year later, and met him for the first time in Charles Street Baptist Church in 1819. In 1821, Mr. Cobb drew up and signed the following document: "By the grace of God, I will never be worth more than fifty thousand dollars. I will give one fourth of the net profits of my business to religious and charitable purposes. If I am ever worth twenty thousand dollars, I will give half of my net income. If I am ever worth thirty thousand dollars, I will give three fourths, and the whole after fifty thousand dollars." To this purpose he religiously adhered. Mr. Gilbert, though he was never permitted to acquire an independent fortune, yet, as a contributor for benevolent purposes, he takes rank with the foremost men of his time. His course towards the poor won for him the title of "Banker for the Poor." Hundreds deposited with him their savings. Mechanics, apprentices, and sewing women, all felt that their money was safe in his hands.

Great numbers came to him for loans — most of them for small amounts. Instances of young men coming to borrow one hundred dollars are remembered. He would turn from his desk, search them with his keen black eye, inquire into the condition of their business and prospects, and then, after ascertaining their wants, would frequently rebuke them for not planning more wisely, when, the lecture over, he would place an adequate sum in their hands, and turn to his work.

Timothy Gilbert's consecration to Christ of all he had deserves mention. We find in his own handwriting a paper which reads as follows: —

"Having, as I trust, through the grace of our Lord Jesus Christ and the influence of his Holy Spirit, been renewed and made an heir of the heavenly inheritance which shall endure forever, and whereas, through the blessing of God upon my efforts, and his guidance in my business affairs, he has given me a portion of this world's goods, and thus, with it the means of doing good to my fellow-men, and at this time is giving indications of still greater enlargement of my pecuniary resources, which, with the examples around me, may tempt me to adopt a more expensive style of living by indulging in luxuries which I now think inconsistent with the claims of my Redeemer, who said, 'Whatsoever ye do, do all to the glory of God,' — I therefore solemnly promise to hold all I now have of this world's goods, as well as my time and my influence, as the Lord's, and to enter into no speculation or engagement in business or expense for myself or my family or relatives, either for travelling, recreation, amusement, or dress, furniture, dwellings, or in any other respect that I do not conscientiously, in the fear of the Lord, think would be in accordance with his will, and meet his favor and approbation, and that I will daily ask him to guide me in all these things, and only prosper me in my business and other plans so far as they are in accordance with his will. And I hereby engage to my holy Redeemer, that I will voluntarily hold all the property I now possess of every kind, as well as myself, subject to his will, not seeking to lay up in store for the future wants of my family, remembering the promise that the 'Lord will provide,' and that if I act the part of a faithful steward, it will be safer to trust in him for our future requirements than in any invested earthly treasure." In like manner he provided that the revenue from his business should be consecrated to the glory of God. Beneath the signature of our lamented brother may be found this sentence: "I heartily concur with my husband in the foregoing. Alice Gilbert, June 19, 1850."

At this time, be it remembered, the profits from his business amounted to some ten to fifteen thousand dollars per annum.

Under date of July 28, 1853, in pencil, it is recorded, "Since the foregoing was written, the Lord has greatly changed my prospects in business, has almost entirely cut off all hope of success, has brought me into circumstances of great pecuniary anxiety and peril, so that my fears are excited lest I shall not be able to pay my just debts, and thereby become bankrupt. Besides all this, the Lord has hidden his face from me, so that I cannot see and behold the face of a reconciled God and Father — cannot get a nearness to him by prayer."

Pause here and consider the facts. In 1850 he was at the zenith of his prosperity. We have seen him laying his all on God's altar. The consecration was made

June 19. We have seen him imperilling life and property in September of the same year in carrying out the principle of the commandment, "Whatsoever ye would that men should do to you, do ye even so to them."

Three years are gone. On the night of March 31, 1852, Tremont Temple was burned. We have not time to dwell upon the gloom which overspread the church, and which overshadowed the deacon's heart. The debt on the original building was being extinguished by the revenue. The church was paying annually twelve hundred dollars towards its extinction. What shall be done? Turn now to another memorandum, and we find, under his own hand, a confirmation of this statement, namely: "Deacon Gilbert, to whose sacrificing labors and untiring zeal this enterprise especially owed its origin, and very much of its success thus far, urged from convictions of duty the necessity of going forward in the work. On the 25th of May, the foundation of the present edifice was laid. The large Temple was first occupied on December 25, 1853. Ten years and eighteen days after the first Temple was dedicated, the second building, grander, larger, and more expensive than the first, was consecrated to the service of Almighty God."

Bear in mind that we have been reading from a paper signed July, 1853. At the time it was written he had placed his all in the scales for God. He had kept his vow. Ruin was before him, but he dared not stop, and the heaviest of all his sorrows came from the withdrawal of the Saviour's face.

Farther on he writes, "I know he is good, and will

be, and that I cannot withhold an acknowledgment of his goodness and righteousness, even if he sends me to perdition."

Picture the scene. There is a man, whose private fortune is threatened, staggering under an additional burden of two hundred thousand dollars, which is increasing every moment, and yet there is no reference to it, or to anything else he has done or attempted.

Again he writes, "If He takes from me everything, I beg of him not to suffer me to complain. All I ask is, that he will permit me to pay my just debts, so that no one to whom I am indebted shall ever suffer by me. But more especially so that the cause of our blessed Master may not be injured or reproached by anything I have done or failed to do. Beyond that I commit myself, my dear and beloved wife, my children, and grandchildren, to the tender care of Him who careth for us all, and who is as kind when he afflicts as when we think he blesses us in worldly matters."

Having emerged into the sunshine, we find this prayer: "O Lord, let it ever be the feeling of my heart to exclaim with David, 'I shall be satisfied when I awake in thy likeness,' perfectly pure and holy. O, let this be my portion, and I ask no other." Again he cries, "'Lift thou up upon me the light of thy countenance, and let me see thy glory.' T. G."

Another memorandum, upon the top of which is written, "*This will explain itself*," must follow here: —

"Fearing that my pecuniary credit may suffer in the event of my sudden decease, as I have reason to fear may happen, and as no one knows the facts of my history as I know them, I make this memorandum, written on the 13th of August, 1860, for the information of friends who may desire to learn the motives by which my life was influenced: —

"When I first began in business with Mr. E. R. Currier I had very moderate expectations, and when I left him and we dissolved, my anticipations were very moderate, and even less than at first.

"But gradually the Lord prospered me; and when, in 1843, because I felt that God called me to do it, I, with others, purchased the Tremont Theatre, and fitted it up for a place of worship, I did it — because I dared not do otherwise — under a deep sense of my pecuniary weakness, and relying wholly upon the Lord. To my surprise the Lord most wonderfully prospered my business, and this enterprise, which was never intended, from first to last, to be of any pecuniary benefit to me individually, or to either of the others associated with me in the undertaking, proved to be a blessing. Without ascribing undue praise to my own exertions, I claim that it is not probable that either or all of the trustees would have undertaken the enterprise if I had not urged them on. Previous to 1852 the Temple was in a fair way to pay its debts from its income, in fifteen years there being but thirty thousand three hundred and twenty-two dollars and eighty-five cents remaining.

"In 1852, when the old building was destroyed, and the question of rebuilding or abandoning the enterprise was to be decided, I again felt a necessity laid upon me to rebuild, as it seemed to me to be practicable, although brother Gould was opposed to it, and brother Shipley only consented providing it could be done without his assuming any personal responsibility beyond what was necessary to make contracts or execute mortgages. Brother Damrell joined me in favoring it, without reservation.

"When completed, the building was found to have cost more than double the amount we had first estimated. This, I found, was more than I could manage, even with the credit of the firm, which was freely used with the consent of Mr. Jameson, who was my only partner at the time. Hence I found it absolutely necessary to sell the property to save all concerned from bankruptcy.

"Our firm had been doing business with ——, of New York, and his indebtedness had become large, which, with the Temple debts, made it seem impossible to stop with him; and therefore we had commenced, and did continue, to renew his paper, and to send him more property, hoping he would reduce his indebtedness to us thereby, until, when he failed, he owed us over thirty thousand dollars; and in the end it was a total loss of not less than twenty-five thousand dollars, most of which would probably have been saved, had we been free from the debts of Tremont Temple, so that we might have refused to renew his paper or send him merchandise. Fearing to so act, lest his paper would all come upon us, we shrank from the responsibility, and bore it as best we could."

Here is a gleam of satisfaction. "Had his failure occurred only a few months sooner, our firm and the whole Temple enterprise would have been involved in hopeless ruin. The Temple debts were assumed by those who took the property off our hands; yet there is no doubt our loss by —— is mainly owing to our connection with the Temple at the same time.

"I leave this as my dying testimony, that the Temple church may know, and all others, that there was no other alternative that I could see, but that the property must be sold to save it from immediate ruin.

"And now our firm owes debts of honor that we at present are wholly unable to pay or secure, owing to our struggles with these embarrassments for years in a dull and oppressed state of trade. We had hoped from year to year that we might again have a return of prosperity, such as characterized us in former years, when our profits ranged from ten to fifteen thousand dollars per annum.

"For more than three years past we have been holding on for some improvement in trade, and all the time we have been losing rather than gaining in our means. We could not stop without loss and suffering to others, and not having lost all hope of bettering our condition, we kept on. If others are finally left to suffer by this means, what I ask of them is, for Christ's sake, to forgive — those of my family and friends who are left destitute, not by extravagant living or worthless expenditures, but by an honest endeavor to rescue my affairs from misfortune and to serve God with my means. I ask for my dear wife and children the sympathy of those who have suffered by me. I have kept nothing back for myself or family, as the Lord knows.

"T. GILBERT.

"August 16, 1860."

Review the scene, and behold that noble form, bent with burdens too heavy to be borne, leaving this record for the church and the world, and praying for forgiveness and asking sympathy for wife and children. There is sublimity in his humility, and grandeur in his patience.

It is something to lose property, but more to lose position. This was his next trial. He was elected a director of the Boylston Bank, October 6, 1854. Three months afterwards, January 9, 1855, he was chosen president, and served the institution with great fidelity until financial difficulties made it his duty to tender his resignation, which was accepted November 19, 1860.

Uncomplainingly he laid down the trust which had been to him a source of mingled pleasure and profit. He bore with him to his retirement the confidence of the directors. They believed him to be incorruptibly honest, kind to a fault, when it was in his power to help a friend, and stern, if not stubborn, when some principle was at stake which demanded protection and support.

CHAPTER IX.

CAUSES WHICH LED TO THE RESIGNATION OF REV. N. COLVER.—MR. GILBERT'S CHARACTER IN A NEW LIGHT.—DEFECTS OF EXTEMPORANEOUS PREACHING.—HIS VIEWS CONCERNING SALARY, AND STUDY, AND VISITING.

HISTORY should be impartial. It seldom is. Biographies should be truthful. They seldom are. The Bible way is the best way. That presents men as they were. Their faults and virtues intermingle. David sinned. We know what were the consequences and the condemnation. Moses made one glaring mistake. It stands forth unconcealed. A story is told of a minister in Virginia who had a horse that had faults. His black servant offered to exchange him. He started on his mission, and chanced to come to a brook where a stranger was watering a horse that delighted the eye of this *connoisseur* of horse flesh. He proposed a trade. The stranger inquired the reason. The servant replied, " This horse has two serious faults." " What are they ? " " One is, my master is a minister, and the horse is white, and every time he goes to preach he gets covered with white hair." " Well, what is the other ? " The African scratched his head, and declared he did not just remember what the other fault was. The man, supposing that it was something like the first, transferred his saddle, and exchanged horses. The next day he brought him back in a wild frenzy, exclaiming, "You black rascal, this horse is blind!" "O, yes," said the servant, "that is the other fault."

In writing biographies many forget the great faults, and only notice the minor ones. A man, as God made him, means something. He is a schoolmaster, and teaches lessons by his faults as well as by his virtues.

The character of Deacon Gilbert had its sharp corners, its obtrusive angles. He had virtues that will keep his memory green for years, and faults that will be remembered until this generation are in their graves. That God's glory was secured by them, or in spite of them, will appear.

He was an earnest advocate for special means of grace for the conversion of souls. His pastor could not toil too earnestly in that direction. His brethren and sisters shared the desire. The church is revival-loving, and in earnest. Clement Drew and Joseph Sherwin, his associate deacons, with Nathaniel Colver, their pastor, were men well calculated to prosecute the harvest work.

Whenever the prospects grew dark for the cause of truth, and the clouds of infidelity began to lower, a day of fasting, and humiliation, and prayer was the alternative to which they gladly turned.

In the support of a pastor he had peculiar, and, we think, erroneous views. It was doubtless a mistake which grew out of the organization of his nature. He believed that the Temple could never be a resort for the rich. He therefore acted upon the principle that it must be made the home for the very poor. He forgot the middling classes that are liberal to a fault, the strangers who cheerfully contribute to the support of the gospel, and the men of brain, of heart, and wealth who could sympathize with his thought, and sacrifice for the promotion of the cause which lay near his heart.

This caused him to feel that the salary of the pastor should never exceed a thousand dollars, and that the residue should be provided for, by voluntary contributions. Hence, while he objected to raising the salary, he gave cheerfully and largely for the education of the children of the pastor, and for such other objects as appealed to his generosity. In religious as in other matters, he was exacting, and so became a trial to his pastor, and oftentimes to his friends. His zeal was quenchless. It never knew abatement. He felt that others should be like him.

He could not understand the necessity which makes it imperative for a minister to seek recreation in other pursuits. Mr. Colver had an inventive genius, and was fond of tools. Lyman Beecher sawed wood. Nathaniel Colver got up designs for spring beds and what not. Deacon Gilbert had little or no sympathy with these pursuits, and would quite likely inquire as to the condition of some sick sister or some inquiring soul, when the pastor was in a glow over some new invention; thus rebuking him in his quiet and provoking way for neglect. Indeed to such an extent did this disposition lead him, that in consequence of it, more than all else, was the first pastor of the Tremont Street Church led to resign. The correspondence is kind, and reveals the characteristics of the two men. The one was an eloquent extemporaneous preacher, who had fought a good fight, who could get up a sermon with but little trouble, who was ever ready for a discussion, who was quick at a retort, witty when not savage, and always open-handed and open-hearted. He did not work three hundred and sixty-five days in a year as he worked on some special occasions. Had he done so, he would never have accomplished those tasks, and ploughed those furrows in Boston which even now ridge the past.

The other was a deacon full of one engrossing thought. Everything must bend to that. Business, pleasure, society, everything was made secondary. His hand was ever on the handle of the bellows. But he never did, and he never could have succeeded without the help of his giant brother, who toiled and rested.

Deacon Gilbert did not appreciate this fact, and so worried the life and disturbed the peace of his pastor. His views in regard to the management of men were, to some extent, erroneous. He had in him a way which sometimes seemed despotic, yet he did not wish to tyrannize. He felt very keenly, and his feelings would reveal themselves in unpropitious ways and at unpropitious times. We do not claim that his pastor was wholly in the right. That the deacon had good and sufficient reasons for his conduct none can deny. It is known that Mr. Colver was not at all times equal. His very temperament made him great for an emergency, and commonplace on ordinary occasions.

He will not agree with this opinion, nor will that class who pride themselves on their ability in extemporaneous speaking; yet it remains true that a man who speaks without a written sermon cannot retain that freshness, that variety, that copiousness in language which the man can who writes.

The extemporaneous preacher runs into ruts, in his divisions of his discourse, in his language, and in the forms of expression, which would be changed at the table with a pen in his hand. On his feet a man will say the most forcible word, and adopt the most forcible form of expression that occurs to him at the moment. It is quite natural for the expression that occurred to him the week previous to occur again. Let Dr. Colver, with his mighty power as an expositor, and, in getting at the "nut" and "cracking it" and "taking out the meat," let him preach before any audience for years, and he will feel the need of the products which are only gleaned on the harvest fields of a pastor's study. This being the state of the case, Deacon Gilbert saw in every new invention of his pastor a barrier to those pursuits which were essential to success.

Another truth deserves to be told. Deacon Gilbert thought that there should be more visiting done by the pastor. The workshop, in his opinion, stood in the way of that, and so, he claimed, inquirers were neglected, and the sick were forgotten. This pained him, and he attempted to remedy the difficulties in his own way. That visiting must be done all admit. That a pastor who has been settled for years in a place, learns to neglect this duty the first of any is also true. Visiting accumulates. It becomes like a mountain. In the Temple it is a very high mountain. To see all is impossible. To satisfy the desire is alike impossible.

To neglect all is the natural result. Again he felt, that, while his pastor was mighty in the Scriptures and in argument, his sermons lacked freshness, because he did not visit and come in contact with the wants of the sick and poor, and that they lacked beauty, because, though the principle of the text was evolved, there was little of the graces of oratory which characterized the periods of an Everett, who polished every sentence with care, and fashioned every passage after some classic model of excellence.

That he was right we do not affirm. That study pays; that ploughing in the closet helps the harvests of the pulpit; that there is no place in the world where culture, fancy, imagination, toil, and erudition yield such dividends as when employed by him who faces from week to week an audience of intelligent, of tired, of hungry men, is abundantly apparent.

The full houses in our large cities are the counterparts of full brains and full hearts. The tricks of oratory, its studied graces, everything that allures, and attracts, and commands when exhibited in the pulpit, meets with a welcome from the pew.

Admitting that this statement of the case is correct, how shall the result be reached? By starving a man, and finding fault with him, or by encouraging him?

There are men who would have gone to Mr. Colver, and said, "Sir, you have mighty powers of oratory. Your imagination is brilliant. Your capacity to visit, to administer to the social wants of the people, and to exert an influence over your ministering brethren is immense. Please bend every energy to the fulfilment of your mission, and we will place your salary where your living need not enter into your thoughts." Adopt such a course, and there is not a minister on earth who knows Christ but would concentrate every power of his mind and heart.

The opposite course was pursued. Advice was given, questions were asked, at times when no man could bear it, as, for instance, when about entering the pulpit or prayer-meeting; and then, to add to all the rest, the salary was raised in spite of, rather than with, the consent of the one who gave the advice. The following gives an insight to his views concerning the subject:

"I have frequently, and that recently, said that you deserved a large salary, as much and more than any of the ministers in the city; for no one that had even two thousand dollars gave away as much as you did, and did not entertain so many of the poor ministers from the country; and, if it could be raised, I should with all my heart advocate your having it. But I have never thought your salary should have been raised above twelve hundred dollars, and have never voted for the increase when made, yet have always said I was willing to pay my proportion even of the advance, and should undoubtedly in some way have done something myself for you, if it had not been raised, as I did while it was only one thousand dollars. I still think it was a mistake in raising it. I well remember that one of the causes that operated in my own mind as an objection to raising it was that I feared it would be the cause of your removal. Knowing that more than nine tenths of all our members did not get even one half of twelve hundred dollars to support their families upon, therefore I believed, and I think the sequel has proved me correct, that it would be harder to get our members who are poor to do what they could if your salary was fifteen hundred dollars than it would if it was twelve hundred dollars or less. And I sincerely and conscientiously think that while our church and congregation are composed of the class it now is and must necessarily be, until the debt of the house is so reduced as to make that easy, the salary should never exceed one thousand dollars. After the debt is provided for, there may be more of a temptation for persons of property to join us. Until then one thousand dollars is the highest salary we ought to think of paying, and, if any can give as individuals besides, let them do so. It was with these views I helped in educating —— when you first came among us, so as to keep the salary at least nominally lower, and experience convinces me that I was correct in my judgment."

These were his views. It is unfortunate that he cherished them, both because of the influence they exerted upon others and upon himself. When it was shown him that Tremont Temple could never be made a success in this way, he readily abandoned the main features of his plan. He saw that it was easier to support a man who can command a large salary than it is to support one of the opposite class. Though the majority of the people worshipping in a free-seated house of worship may be poor, it does not follow that they are mean. The young men who throng the galleries are ever ready to respond to appeals for aid, as was repeatedly shown during the war. They spend money for pleasure, for society, and are quite as willing, if not more willing, to consecrate a portion of their earnings to the support of the cause of Christ.

The character of the congregation seems not to have been understood. When, under the new *régime*, it was proposed to raise the large proportion of the salary by subscription, none were more surprised than were the oldest worshippers at the Temple when the returns came in which provided an income of over five thousand dollars to meet current expenses. When the claims of societies which had hitherto been ignored were presented, the subscriptions in their behalf reached a large sum. When the echoes of the guns at Antietam disturbed the quiet of the Sabbath, and caused the cry to run from church to church, that worship should be suspended, and that the worshippers should betake themselves to the preparation of lint, Tremont Temple was thrown open, and the product of the labor there bestowed found its way earliest to the battle-field. Afterwards, when Washington was beleaguered with foes, and the call came for minute men for action, the pastor explained the want, and two hundred men before Monday noon were enrolled for action. When the Christian Commission issued their call for aid, the subscription of the Temple stood grandly forth among the larger contributions for that worthy object. These facts reveal the character of the congregation, and prove that they can sustain any man who commands their respect and love. The generous policy begets a generous spirit. It is no more difficult to make it fashionable to give than it is to make it popular to withhold. Mr. Gilbert was liberal to a fault himself, but had learned to doubt the liberality of others. When at last the church rallied round the banner, and placed their choicest gifts on

God's altar, and pledged their pastor a generous support, and led off in all generous acts and deeds, none were happier, and none were in advance of Timothy Gilbert. His smiling face, his joyous speech, and thankful prayers revealed his appreciation of God's goodness to the Temple of his love and the people of his choice.

CHAPTER X.

RESIGNATION OF REV. NATHANIEL COLVER. — TREMONT TEMPLE BURNT. — A DESCRIPTION OF THE NEW TEMPLE. — DEACON GILBERT'S VIEW OF THE ENTERPRISE.

IN 1852 Nathaniel Colver tendered his resignation as pastor of the Tremont Street Church. On the 30th of March he sent away his goods to Abington, and came to pass the night at the house of Deacon Gilbert. That night, at one o'clock, the bells rang the alarm for fire, and before four o'clock the Tremont Temple was in ruins.

"Who fathoms the Eternal Thought?
Who talks of scheme and plan?
The Lord is God. He needeth not
The poor device of man."

Turning to the diary of Deacon Gilbert we naturally look for a murmur. We find it not. Is there no compunction of conscience? None. What was right yesterday is right to-day. Here is the record: —

"This morning, about one o'clock, Tremont Temple took fire, and was a heap of ruins by four A. M. Went down in the forenoon to T. Gould's, and met with trustees. — Evening. Church met at my house — from forty to fifty present."

Thursday he agitates the question of rebuilding. Friday the question is considered in a full meeting. Sabbath, Rev. N. Colver preaches his farewell sermon, in Marlboro' Chapel. Now begins his march from bank to insurance office, from trustees to architect. His private business is neglected, and all for this.

On Wednesday, April 7, the church hold a church meeting at his house, and vote to refer the matter of rebuilding the Temple to the trustees. What say the trustees? Here is the record in his own hand, and it shows that while others faltered he moved on : —

" Brother Gould was opposed to it. Brother Shipley only consented providing it could be done without his assuming any personal responsibility beyond what was necessary to make contracts and execute mortgages. Brother Damrell joined me in favoring it without reservation."

This encouraged him. Day after day he is moving from point to point; now attending to the clearing away of the ruins, now cheering on the halting, now arranging his affairs with the bank and consulting with his lawyer. On May 25 we find this entry: " This day commenced laying foundation to the new Tremont Temple."

On the 25th of August, 1852, Deacon S. G. Shipley died; and from this time his burdens increased. Each day you can see the walls are rising. He holds the measure and marks the progress made. On December 25, 1853, the Tremont Temple was consecrated to public worship. A description of this building furnishes a bird's eye view of the achievement won. Let us begin with

The Exterior of the Tremont Temple.

Immediately opposite the Tremont House — and so near it that, when the walls of the old Temple fell into the street, the front of the hotel had a narrow escape — stands "The Stranger's Sabbath Home." Of a rich and warm brown tint, produced by a coating of mastic, it presents a peculiarly substantial and elegant frontage. It is seventy-five feet in height, and with the exception of ten feet by sixty-eight, which is left open on the north side for light, the building covers an area of thirteen thousand feet.

The walls are massive and of great strength, varying in thickness from thirty-six inches to sixteen inches, and, in accordance with the most approved mode of building, are hollow. This, of course, insures great proportional strength, dry inside walls, a saving in furring and lathing by admitting of plastering upon the bricks, a prevention of the ravages of vermin, and greater resonance and adaptation to music in the walls of the large halls. It will be at once evident that this method, also, to a very considerable extent, obviates all danger of fire spreading, as it often does, and did to the destruction of the old Temple, between the plastering and the wall. Wherever, in the new building, it has been found necessary to use furring and plastering, layers of brick have been placed to cut off all chance of fire spreading between the plastering from one story to another. The floors, too, have, as we shall, by and by, more particularly notice, a thick coating of mortar between the upper and under courses of boards, as a protection against the spread of fire, and to prevent the transmission of sound.

The summit of the Temple is crowned by a lofty cupola, and under it runs a bold and handsomely designed cornice. Immediately below the cornice are five arched recesses or niches, and under these the same number of lofty windows that light the front apartments, to be hereafter described. At the street level are four fine stores. In the centre is the principal entrance door, painted in imitation of dark oak. The whole external appearance is imposing, and the building is worthy of the city of which it is at once an ornament and a convenience.

The Entrance.

Passing through the great central door-way, we find ourselves in a spacious lobby or entrance hall. On the first floor we observe, on our right, and on the first landing, the ticket office, and a broad flight of stairs on either hand, each of which, at its summit, terminates in a landing, from whence, to right and left, diverge two flights of similar staircases, one landing you in the centre of the main hall, and the other to the rear part and the gallery.

The Main Hall,

Or *The* Temple, as many style it from long-accustomed habit, although, in fact, it forms but one portion of it, is a commodious and magnificent audience-room. The utter absence of gilding and coloring on its walls renders it far more imposing and grand in appearance than if it had been elaborately ornamented with auriferous and chromatic splendors. The following are its dimensions: It is one hundred and twenty-four feet long, seventy-two feet wide, and fifty feet high. Around the sides of it runs a gallery supported on trusses, so that no pillars intervene between the spectator and the platform to obstruct the view. The front of this gallery is balustraded, and by this means a very neat and uniform effect is secured. The side galleries project over the aisles below about seven feet. They are fitted with rows of nicely cushioned and comfortable seats, and are not so high as to render the ascent to them wearisome in the least degree. The front gallery, though it projects into the hall only ten feet, extends back far enough to give it more than three times that depth, and when filled with spectators, as it is on the Sabbath from week to week, presents a truly magnificent spectacle.

Directly opposite this gallery is the platform, with its gracefully panelled, semicircular front. This platform, covered with a neat oil-cloth, communicates with the side galleries by a few steps, for the convenience of the choir. There are also several avenues of communication from the platform to the apartments, dressing-rooms, &c., behind, which are exceedingly convenient, and are far superior to the places of exit and entrance from, and to, any other place of the kind that we have ever seen.

From the front of the platform the floor of the hall gradually rises, so as to afford every person in the hall a full and unobstructed view of the speakers or vocalists, as the case may be. The seats in the galleries rise in like manner. The seats on the hall floor are admirably arranged in a semicircular form from the front of the platform, so that every face is directed towards the speaker or singer. They are numbered uniformly, have iron ends, are capped with mahogany, and are completely cushioned with a drab-colored material. Each slip is capable of containing ten or twelve persons, with an aisle at each extremity, and open from end to end.

The side walls of the hall are very beautifully ornamented in panels, arched and decorated with circular ornaments, which it would be difficult properly to describe without the aid of accompanying drawings; but as views of the interior of the Temple have become common, the omission here will be of little consequence. As we intimated, there is no fancy coloring; it is a decorated and relieved surface of dead white, and the effect, lighted as it is from above by large panes of rough plate glass, is beautifully chaste. The only color observable in the hall is the purple screen behind the diamond open-work at the back of the platform, and which forms a screen in front of the organ. The effect of this solitary "bit" of coloring is remarkably fine.

The ceiling is very finely designed in squares, at the intersections of which are twenty-eight gas-burners, which, with strong reflectors, and a chandelier over the orchestra, shed a mellow but ample light over the hall. By this arrangement, the air, heated by innumerable jets of gas, is got rid of, and the lights themselves act as most efficient ventilators. The eyes are likewise protected from glare; and should an escape of gas take place, from its levity it passes up through shafts to the outside, and does not contaminate the atmosphere below. Under the galleries are common burners. There are for day illuminations twelve immense plates of glass, ten feet long by four feet wide, placed in the ceiling in the spring of the arch, and open directly to the outer light, and sixteen smaller ones under the galleries.

The whole of the flooring of the hall, in the galleries, the body of it, and of the platform, consists of two layers of boards, with the interstices between them filled by a thick bed of mortar. The advantages of this, in an acoustical point of view, must be obvious to all. Another advantage is, that the applause made by the audience in this great hall does not disturb the people who may at the same time be holding a meeting in the other hall below — a very important consideration. Now, on the occasion of an outburst of enthusiasm above, only a slight indication thereof is heard in the lesser hall.

There are eight flights of stairs leading from the floors of the main hall, and four from the galleries, the aggregate width of which is over fifty feet.

Of the ventilation of this great hall we shall speak under its appropriate head. We would, however, direct attention to the ingenious contrivance at the back of the front gallery, by means of which the foul air is carried off.

Office Entrance and Private Passage to the Halls.

On the south side of the building is an entrance-way about seven feet wide, under the head of offices, where also may be seen the names of the occupants and the number of their rooms, which leads to all the departments of the Temple. When the public halls are not occupied, access can be had to any of the apartments through the main entrance, if desired, but at all times through this passage way.

Boston Young Men's Christian Association.

These beautiful rooms are up one flight of stairs, and are admirably adapted for their present uses and occupants, and are rented by the Association for sixteen hundred dollars per annum, though it is estimated that they are worth, at least, twenty-five hundred dollars; but the Temple is controlled by a society who were very desirous that a religious association should occupy them.

The committee of the Young Men's Christian Association, in a late report, say, "We are now in a building well known, easily found, and convenient of access to all the city. We have halls for our lectures in the same building, and on very favorable terms. We are only one story from the ground. We have a large reading-room, a library-room, and three other rooms, for prayer meetings, committees, &c. The central situation of these rooms will also enable the committee to carry out a plan they have matured, for bringing the clergymen of our city more to the rooms, and making them better acquainted with each other. The plan is, to have the mail matter of all our clergymen brought to our rooms at all suitable times of the day, and there distributed into boxes, for each one; so that the clergy can get it at that place as conveniently as at the Post

Office, while, at the same time, they can have the advantages of the reading-room, and of seeing each other daily. They can also answer their letters there, the proper conveniences being always ready. We shall thus become a sort of religious exchange — the head-quarters of all the clergy, not only of our city, but of New England. The clergymen generally are glad to come into the arrangement, and we hope for good results to our society and to Christian union from it." *

On entering this suit of rooms, we first come to that one occupied as a library. Behind substantial railings are shelves filled with books. Next to that is a large and handsomely furnished reading-room, where, on convenient stands, are arranged various newspapers; and on the walls hang superb engravings, mostly of scriptural subjects. On the table lie magazines and journals, and in the most comfortable of chairs their contents may be studied.

Beyond the reading-room is a committee-room, and a room in which religious services are held weekly. The whole of the arrangements, it must be perceived, are admirable. This suit, then, consists of a central room, forty-eight feet long by thirty feet wide, with two side rooms, each about thirty feet by fifteen, and two smaller rooms, about fifteen feet by seven, with closets and other conveniences. These rooms extend entirely across the front of the building, and open upon a balcony which commands a very extensive view.

Altogether it would be difficult to find a more convenient and beautiful suit of rooms in our city, for the

* This scheme has been abandoned.

purposes of the Association. Back of these, on the same story, are eight large and fine rooms, averaging about twenty-six feet by sixteen, well lighted, and furnished with closets and other conveniences. Over the rooms of the Christian Association, front, there are five rooms of good size, about twenty-five by fifteen feet, suitable for artists; and at the sides, over the stairways, there are six other similar rooms.

The organ was built by Messrs. Hook, whose reputation forms a sufficient guarantee for the excellence of the instrument.

Let us leave now the splendid great hall, and pay a visit to

The Meionaon,

The main entrance to which is through the northerly passage way, opposite the doors of the Tremont House; this avenue is about seven feet wide. The southerly passage way, elsewhere described, serves as an outlet from this Lesser Temple.

Perhaps the reader, who may not have been initiated into the mysteries of Greek literature, may thank us for a definition of this strange-looking word, *Meionaon*. It is so called from two Greek words; *meion*, signifying *less*, *smaller*, and *naon*, *temple* — lesser temple. It should be pronounced mi-o-na-on. This lesser temple is situated back from the street, and directly under the great hall. It is seventy-two feet long by fifty-two feet wide, and about twenty-five and a half feet high: not so elaborately adorned as its neighbor overhead, this hall is rented by the church, and is used for the Sabbath school and weekly meetings.

The Vestry.

In front of this hall, and on the same level, is a large and very commodious vestry, having two entrances, opposite which is the Social Hall, or large parlor, used by the church for social purposes, and where the leading laymen of the denomination meet monthly with invited guests, to greet each other as brethren in the Lord, and consult together regarding the general interests of the denomination.

Fire-Room.

Outside the main wall of the building, and below the level of the street, is what is called the fire-room. This may be termed the centre of that great circulating system by means of which the building is heated. Here is a large cylindrical boiler, from which pipes proceed and ramify in all directions over the vast building; the water, after it has performed its "mission," being brought back again to be re-heated and re-sent upon its round. A steam pump is here erected to supply the boiler, &c.

Ventilation.

Perhaps the most noticeable feature in the Tremont Temple is the thorough and perfect manner in which it is warmed and ventilated, the trustees being deeply impressed with the importance of providing a hall for the use of the public, that should, *in all respects*, be comfortable and agreeable, determined to spare no pains or expense in having the ventilation of the rooms thorough, and the temperature such as the most delicate invalid or robust citizen could not find fault with. In order to render the building secure against fire, it seemed desirable to warm the entire establishment, containing no less than thirty rooms, besides the great hall, with a single fire. To do this, that mighty agent, *steam*, was called upon ; and well and handsomely does it respond. A large boiler, in a remote corner of the premises, not under the main building, and which we have before referred to, generates steam, which is carried through the conducting pipes into brick chambers of various shapes and sizes, all filled with iron pipes. Into these chambers, or reservoirs of heat, cold air is introduced through large conductors, whose external terminations are near the top of the building, remote from the dust and noxious vapors of the street. After having received its proper degree of warmth, and been rectified in its hygrometric qualities, this air is admitted, through large trellised openings, to the halls and other apartments.

Into some of the rooms the steam pipes are introduced directly, and after coiling themselves around the room a few times, go on their way into other rooms. Thus each room is warmed independently of the others. Indeed, the supply of heat to all the rooms and various parts of the building, is placed under the most perfect control by means of *valves*, so that in each room the temperature may be graduated with mathematical accuracy, without at all interfering with the temperature of any other room.

In order to make the ventilation copious and reliable, there are large air shafts over flues at the corners of the hall, terminating at the roof, through which, by means of steam heat, a constant upward current is obtained; and into these shafts, or flues, all the heated and impure air of the room is constantly discharged, so that, though the great hall may be packed with human beings, yet the constant introduction of fresh, warm, pure air, floating over the audience like a gentle zephyr of the tropics, and the as constant ejection of impure air, cause the atmosphere of the rooms to have a delightful freshness and elasticity.

As there is no red-hot iron to burn the air before it enters the room, as is generally the case with hot-air furnaces, and as the steam pipes afford an admirable facility for purifying the air, as well as heating it, the temperature of the room is not unlike that of a green-house, filled with fragrant plants. And what are human beings, with lungs of the most delicate organization, but plants of a heavenly growth? too often, alas, "nipped in the bûd" by being obliged to breathe an atmosphere deprived of its vitality by fire, or poisoned by impurity! Is it not strange that so little attention has been paid to this system of combining heat and ventilation for our public buildings?

Too much praise cannot be awarded to the parties by whom this work in the Tremont Temple was planned and executed — Messrs. James J. Walworth & Co. It is one more proof of the success which seems to have invariably attended their efforts in this novel and interesting method of heating, and they have certainly succeeded in rendering the Tremont Temple the most comfortable, as it is the most unique and beautiful, room of the kind, in our city.

Ante-rooms, &c.

Both the large and small halls have attached to them ante-rooms, where, on the occasion of concerts, or other exhibitions, the vocalists or performers may dress or repose. These are fitted up with every requisite that can be imagined. Those for ladies are situated on one side of the platform, and for gentlemen on the other, and all needful privacy is secured. There are many other apartments in the building, well situated for artists and dentists.

The Cupola.

In making our way thither, we travel over the ceiling of the great hall, dropping our heads as we pass beneath roof and rafter, to save our hat and skull, and beholding beneath our feet a great net-work of gas-piping connected with the burners of the hall under us. In long rows are square ventilators, which discharge their streams of vitiated air on the outside.

The cupola forms a spacious observatory, glazed all round, and from every window is obtained a charming view, the whole forming one of the most superb panoramas that we ever witnessed. From this elevated spot may be seen the adjacent villages and towns, the harbor and its islands, the city institutions, churches, houses, and shipping. In short, the whole city and its vicinity lie at our feet.

General Survey.

We have thus gone through this vast building, but it would be impossible to give the entire details of every part in a sketch of this kind; nor is it necessary. It would be an unpardonable omission, however, did we omit to state that the skilful architect, under whose direction it has arisen, is Mr. William Washburn — a gentleman well known for great ability in his difficult profession.

Everything used in the construction of the Temple appears to be of the best kind. The chief carpenter work and finishing was done by George Nowell & Co.; the painting by Mr. Thaddeus Stone; and the plaster, stucco, and mastic work outside, by Mr. Joseph Kingsley; mason work by Carlton Parker.

Statistics of Tremont Temple.

The following particulars, respecting the origin and financial arrangements of this great building, are authentic, and cannot fail to be of interest.

The original object of those who have been most interested in the Tremont Temple enterprise has been, and still is, to keep open a place of public worship on the Sabbath, with free seats, for the young persons who are constantly coming to the city for employment, a large portion of whom are unable to procure seats in other churches, and therefore spend their Sabbaths by walking about the city and its vicinity, and in that way coming in contact with the idle and the vicious, are drawn into the paths of vice, and, by degrees, to crime, degradation, and ruin. It is mainly to save this class that this place is opened, and also for the strangers who visit it for temporary purposes.

But the enterprise has become of much greater importance, prospectively, by the building of the new Temple, as may be seen by the following statement: —

The estimated income from the present stores and offices, together with the income of the large halls, will not be likely to fall short of ten or twelve thousand dollars per annum, over the current expenses. This, when all the debts are paid, is all to be given away for charitable objects, not less than one half of which *must* be expended in the city, for the wants of the poor, and the other half may be expended in the same way, or for other objects specified in the deed of trust by which it is held. It is estimated that the income will pay all current expenses, and the interest on one hundred thousand dollars, to which it is the purpose of the trustees to reduce the debt, and leave a sinking fund of not less than four thousand dollars per annum, which will pay the whole debt in less than twenty years; and this estimate is made, leaving the gratuitous use of the parts occupied for religious worship out from the calculation, thus, from this time, providing a large, central, and inviting place of worship, with seats free, all lighted, warmed, and kept in repair, and, prospectively (probably within twenty years), providing more than the interest of a two hundred thousand dollar fund to feed the hungry, to clothe the naked, to supply the wants of the destitute, for annual distribution, and all this without any person giving for such a fund.

It is, however, provided in the trust deed, that any donations that may be made shall be appropriated for the extinguishment of the debts, unless otherwise ordered by the donors.

Cost of Building and Furniture.

The cost of the building, including heating apparatus by steam, was not far from one hundred and sixty thousand dollars, and the furniture, including organs, not far from fifteen thousand dollars.

Management of the Property.

The property is under the entire and absolute control of trustees, elected annually by representatives of Baptist churches, who are controlled by the provisions of the trust deed.

The Union Temple Church are bound by the provisions of the deed forever to maintain public worship on the Sabbath, with free seats, without using any part of this income for that purpose; and if they do not so maintain public worship, a minority of said church are authorized to organize for that purpose, and enjoy the benefit of this trust in the same manner.

"We should be sorry to close this brief notice of the Tremont Temple without specially alluding to the church, which, in fact, formed the *nucleus* of the entire fabric."

"In a city like Boston, the importance of such an institution cannot well be overrated. It not unfrequently happens that a stranger in the city, on the Sabbath day, finds it no very easy matter to obtain a sitting in one of our crowded places of worship; and we ourselves, on more than one occasion, have had to stand, either lingering in the aisle until our legs ached, before the pew-opener deigned to notice us, or to remain on our feet during an entire service. We have heard that a visitor to a certain church not a hundred miles from the city of Boston, once, on finding that no one heeded him as he stood in the aisle, left the building and returned with a chair, on which he calmly rested himself—a quiet commentary on the want of common civility on the part of the officials. Now, all such inconveniences as these may very easily be avoided by going to the church in Tremont Temple, where every seat is free to whoever may choose to take it."

"A free church! There is something noble and beautiful in the very sound! Free as air—free as ocean waves—free as the everlasting gospel which is preached within its walls! Free to all! As none were exempted in the great invitation of the Saviour, so to this free church all are invited and are welcome. No grim sexton stands in the aisle, to survey you from head to foot as you stand waiting his pleasure, and unless you be genteel, will not let you come "between the wind and his nobility," or usher you into a pew. No purse-proud occupant of a seat that he only enjoys, though there be room and to spare for half a dozen more, looks complacently at you as he lolls on his cushions; but instead of this, you walk quietly to any unoccupied place, and take it as your right. This is as it should be; and well may the strangers in Boston bless the benevolence of those who fitted up this beautiful place for their accommodation." *

Mr. G.'s diary and private correspondence give us

* The above description is in part taken from an article by George W. Bungay, first published in the "Waverley Magazine and Literary Messenger."

an insight to the burdens imposed upon him, and the loss he sustained in the death of Deacon Shipley.

Impressed by the favoring providences which helped him in carrying forward his work, tried by the course pursued by the architect, disappointed if not dejected by the manner in which the bills exceeded the bids, he finds relief and comfort alone at the throne of grace.

In 1853 the Temple was finished and dedicated, and the following paper was written in July of the same year, and left as an evidence of his desires and wishes regarding the use to be made of it: —

"I, Timothy Gilbert, having been the principal instrument that the Lord has used in purchasing, refitting, and again in rebuilding, the Tremont Temple, do hereby leave upon record my desires and wishes concerning the same, and what I believe to be the will of God, who has so signally blessed and favored the enterprise from its commencement. And I hereby wish it to be remembered that this is not the work of Timothy Gilbert, he being only the instrument in the hands of God, used to carry forward His own benevolent designs, and that the Tremont Street Church have no cause to exult, but rather to inquire, 'Lord, what wilt thou have us to do?' for never was there a church placed under greater responsibilities than devolve upon this people, who are called upon, by their position and the circumstances which environ them, to see to it that the whole enterprise shall be carried on for the advancement of the cause of truth and morality, and not for the pecuniary benefit or honor of any individual or individuals; and I hereby leave this as my solemn conviction, that whenever the time shall come when no one will carry on this enterprise for the love they bear to the cause of Christ and without pecuniary reward, then the glory of Tremont Temple will have departed. Then let the church clothe themselves with sackcloth, and fast and pray until the Lord will raise up and qualify one or more to do this work, and to say, 'Lord, here am I; take me, and use me for that service;' otherwise darkness will overshadow the enterprise from that time forward. Let the church, having the benefit of this trust, guard against even indulging for a moment the desire or wish to use any part of the income for the ordinary support of a pastor, lest that wish or desire should be seen, by Him who looks on the heart, to grow out of the selfish desire to shirk the burdens of the Lord's house, and thus make them guilty of wishing to offer to the Lord 'that which costs them nothing.' Let the church adhere to the conditions of the charter or deed; and whenever a doubt arises as to its meaning and intent, let them construe it in favor of the poor who are to be benefited by the income, and not to relieve themselves from the slightest responsibility.

"Let them also conscientiously consider this in all the uses they may make of the income, in all alterations and repairs, in letting or refusing to let, and act conformably to the principle that they are stewards of the Lord's family, and must give an account to Him who put them into the stewardship. Let every one who shall undertake to steady the ark or conduct the enterprise, by their own skill, or strength, or wisdom, without consulting the Lord, be as Uzzah, if it should be myself. Let every one who shall dare to put their hands to it, remember that it is *a holy enterprise*, begun and carried on by a holy God; that its past success is all of Him, and if ultimately successful, all the glory will legitimately belong to Him, and to no earthly instrument whatever. And I hereby leave it to be remembered and acted upon by all who may speak of me, or mention my name in connection with it, when I am dead, that the honor of my Lord and Saviour will be tarnished, and his frown called down upon every attempt to give the glory to me or to any other human being. After my decease, let what I have written on this, the 10th day of July, 1853, be faithfully considered, and may the Lord add his blessing."

CHAPTER XI.

THE TREMONT TEMPLE ENTERPRISE IMPERILLED. — THE PROPERTY OFFERED FOR SALE. — THE ORGANIZATION OF THE EVANGELICAL BAPTIST BENEVOLENT AND MISSIONARY SOCIETY. — THE SKY CLEARING. — MR. GILBERT'S HOPES BRIGHTENING. — LETTER OF REV. D. C. EDDY, D. D.

THE years 1854 and 1855 are thick with shadows. In the political world there were Kansas excitements, the trial of Burns, his rendition to slavery in the presence of a vast concourse of people, the state militia looking on, and the deacon "agonizing over the triumphs of slavery."

In the church all was dark. The Temple, capable of accommodating a vast congregation, was never full; the prayer meetings were thinly attended; the brethren, feeling to repine at the loss sustained by the resignation of Dr. Colver, and not rallying as one man about the new pastor, failed to sympathize with him in his views, aims, or plans; while, financially, the sky was growing dark rather than bright, and the burdens Mr. Gilbert bore threatened to ingulf him in ruin.

The year 1855 furnished the turning point in the history of the Temple. The church were discouraged. They who had given their prayers and pecuniary aid, to a limited extent, tired of the burden, and desiring to avail themselves of the money that would accrue to them from the sale of the property, opposed Mr. Gilbert's plans and thwarted his purposes. On Wednesday, May 30, 1855, Rev. T. C. Jameson tendered his resignation, and Deacon Gilbert made the attempt to dissolve his connection with a church in which, for many years, he had borne a very prominent part.

The Sabbaths that followed must have been Sabbaths of peculiar experiences. He goes to Merrimack Street, to Rowe Street, to Somerset Street, to Brookline, and, at last, September 2, 1855, becomes a member of the First Baptist Church, where he remained until 1859, when, difficulties having been removed, he saw his way clear to resume his work in the field of his early love and choice.

His removal from the Tremont Street Church severed one of the strong ties that bound him to the enterprise. His pecuniary liabilities made it imperative that something be done for his relief. The Temple was offered for sale first to his own denomination, it being understood, in case of their failure to purchase it, that the Congregationalists stood ready to take the property.

At this stage of affairs one of the trustees refused to convey the property to the denomination, because of his desire to secure a fund for the church out of the estate. Concerning this Mr. Gilbert writes, that "however desirable this may be for the church, he is unwilling that it shall interfere with the original design, which has been to secure the property for the cause of evangelical religion and morality, and for the benefit of the poor in the city of Boston."

At this time the crisis was reached. The church opposed the sale of the Temple, because of their vested rights. The deacon, having concluded to sell the property, hoped to find a purchaser in the Baptist denomination. In case of failure in that quarter, he had entered into negotiations with the Orthodox Congregationalists. The church became alarmed, and sent for Dr. Colver. The excitement seemed to rouse the denomination. A glance at the figures shows that the church had received more than an adequate return for the amount invested, and that it was better for them to suffer than to have the property pass beyond the control of evangelical Christians.

"Man's extremity is God's opportunity." It was well that the property should be taken out of the hands of the church, and placed in the care of a board of trustees chosen by ballot and representing the different churches in Boston and vicinity.

The Tremont Temple was conceived as a missionary enterprise, designed to furnish the gospel to the spiritually destitute in the city, and to create a fund to aid in giving the gospel to the spiritually destitute elsewhere.

Fears were justly entertained that this interest would be swallowed up by the Roman Catholic church. The future of Boston seemed to be involved in the action of the denomination. The church were unequal to the task. They were poor. It is probably true that no matter how loud individuals may be in their professions of regard for the work to be done in such a place, yet very few of what are called leading men and their families will join the church. Now and then a powerful impression of duty or strong personal considerations will bring such help, but not often.

"The heterogeneous character of the congregation; the uncertainty as to where one will sit, or whether he will sit with his family, or whether, indeed, he will not have to stand up; the lack of the numberless associations which make the sanctuary a religious *home* — dearest and sweetest home sometimes in all the world; the scarcity of families; and the lack of society and friendly communion, — all these, whether properly or not, tend to keep back the rich."

This is the charge. The conduct of Christian men should disprove it if it be not already disproved. If ordinary family churches need judicious, sagacious, benevolent, devoted, and directing spirits, who, by common consent, are denominated "leading men," whom the people love to follow, how much more does this church need them! No one can look at the strangers gathered from all lands at each service, without seeing the necessity of representative men forming a stated part of the congregations. No one can look upon the hundreds of young men and women who come as strangers, and need the hand of welcome to be extended to them by the church of God on the threshold of their new life, without being impressed by the want of men of character and influence to greet and guide them. Such a threshold the "Stranger's Sabbath Home" ought to become. Nowhere else does influence tell to such advantage. It is impossible to make the poor herd together. In God's house the rich and poor should meet together. Young men wish to meet their employers outside of their places of business. If merchants care for the commercial future of the city in which they live, they cannot afford to overlook Tremont Temple, or keep aloof from it, for, by so doing, they separate themselves from the young men who look up to them for example and guidance. If Christian men care for the future character of their denomination, they cannot afford to neglect such instrumentalities of usefulness. They owe it to God, to the country, to the young men that are being influenced by them, and to him who ministers to the people in holy things, to give their countenance to, and grace with their presence, such places of popular resort. Every public speaker understands the influence exerted by a man of mark and character forming a part of the congregation. It is said that the entrance of Daniel Webster into a theatre changed the character of the play. The actors forgot the pit and thought of the statesman instead.

Perhaps it ought not to be so, but it is so. The influence of the pew is felt in the pulpit as much as the influence of the pulpit is felt in the pew. Notwithstanding this, from the causes indicated, the number of influential and leading men will never be large in such a place, and those that come will have enough to do without being forced to guide a miscellaneous church made up of youths, of the poor and of the middling classes, who are grand as helpers in winning souls, but who are not familiar with the management of large parochial trusts. Better, by far, is it to have the property held by trustees connected with other churches, who will sympathize with the work, take an interest in the congregation, as well as in the property, and who will act for the good of the denomination and the glory of God, and leave the church to reap for Christ. This all looks plain now, but it seemed uncertain ground in 1855. Experience has proven that such a church ought to have just as little as possible to do with legislating, with planning, with management. The best government is that which governs least. Surely, no one can gaze upon the assembled thousands in the congregations on the Sabbath, or upon the hundreds gathered in the Sabbath schools and Bible classes, without feeling that a work is before the church worthy of an angel's powers.

Entertaining these views, we tread with delight the path which seemed so full of thorns, because from every stem there has come forth a full-blown rose.

A meeting of the prominent members of the Baptist denomination in this city and vicinity was called, and a public meeting was held in the Meionaon, March 1, 1855.

This meeting deemed it desirable to secure the estate to the denomination, and appointed a committee for this purpose. Other meetings were held, but, for various reasons, without being able to accomplish the end desired. As there appeared to be no immediate prospect of relief, the property was afterwards advertised to be sold by public auction, on the 20th of June following; but the sale was postponed to carry out an arrangement, which was being made, to place the property, temporaily, in the hands of thirty-seven individuals, until subscriptions could be obtained for its purchase, with a view of conveying it to a society, to be called the Evangelical Baptist Benevolent and Missionary Society.

In accordance with this arrangement, it was conveyed by deed, dated June 28, 1855, to Thomas Richardson, Frederick Gould, J. W. Converse, G. W. Chipman, and J. W. Merrill, as trustees, and the sum of thirty-six thousand seven hundred and eleven dollars and three cents over and above its outstanding liabilities was paid therefor.

An act of incorporation was secured in 1857 for an association known as the Evangelical Baptist Benevolent and Missionary Society, to be located in the city of Boston, for the purpose of securing the constant maintenance in said Boston of evangelical preaching for the young and the destitute, with free seats; for the employment of colporteur and missionary laborers in Boston and elsewhere; for the purpose of providing suitable central apartments to other and kindred benevolent and missionary societies; and for the general purpose of ministering to the spiritual wants of the needy and destitute, with the right of holding real and personal estate to the amount of three hundred and fifty thousand dollars, which property, and the net income thereof after the same has been paid for, shall be appropriated exclusively for the purposes in this act specified, and the same shall be exempted from taxation.

The society was organized May 11, 1858, and on the 14th of June the constitution was adopted, and at a subsequent meeting the following officers were elected:—

President.

James W. Converse.

Secretary.

Joseph Story.

Treasurer.

J. Warren Merrill.

Directors.

Thomas Richardson, *Boston.*
George W. Chipman, "
Timothy Gilbert, "
Charles D. Gould, "
Asa Wilbur, "
George S. Dexter, "
Charles S. Kendall, "
Jesse Tirrell, "
J. W. Converse, *Jamaica Plain.*
George W. Little, *Charlestown.*
Frederick Gould, *Cambridge.*
William H. Jameson, *Brookline.*
William A. Bowdlear, *Roxbury.*

Auditors.

Joshua Loring, *Chelsea.*
Joshua Lincoln, *Roxbury.*

A lease was executed December 6, 1858, "granting the Tremont Street Baptist Church and Society the use of the great hall, with the organ and furniture therein, during the daytime on Sundays, as a place of public worship; and also basement rooms for vestry and Sabbath school; the church agreeing to maintain public worship on the Sabbath, with free seats, and to support a good and efficient pastor, who shall be considered creditable to the denomination, and such as shall be so considered by the Baptist churches in the city of Boston and the adjoining cities and towns of Dorchester, Roxbury, Brookline, Cambridge, Charlestown, and Chelsea; and that the church shall hold and maintain the doctrines of the evangelical Baptist churches in said cities and towns. Either of the Baptist churches in said cities and towns may at any time call a council, to be composed of two members from such churches — not less than a majority of the whole number — as may choose to send delegates, to inquire whether the church has broken any of these covenants; and if the council so chosen shall decide that the church has failed to comply with any of the covenants, then this lease shall cease. In case of a sale of the estate, this lease is null and void; and the amount realized from the sale, after paying the cost of the same to this corporation, with interest, charges, and expenses, shall be paid over to said church, which amount shall be held in trust by the deacons of said church, for the purpose of building a new place of worship, or to be appropriated to some other religious or charitable object by said church."

The obligations of the denomination to those brethren who stepped forward and by their individual credit, as well as by their contributions, saved the enterprise from irretrievable ruin, cannot be over-estimated. At a time when another denomination stood ready, money in hand, to purchase the Temple, and make it the centre of influence and the source of power, then there were found men, who had been blessed of God with property, who, without delay, pledged their fortunes and gave their influence to serve a denomination which had furnished them with a spiritual home. The friends remember, in like manner, the efforts of that young man who became pastor in the autumn of 1855, whose preaching soon gathered large congregations, and whose appeals for aid in Boston and vicinity resulted in raising forty thousand dollars, with which the floating debt was paid, and without which the property could not have been secured.

From 1858 to 1862 the church acted independently of the Board in the selection of the pastor. In the mean time stories prejudicial to the standing and character of the minister were circulated. After his resignation it was felt to be desirable that an understanding between the church and the Board of Directors should be entered into. Hence in 1862 a meeting was called, and a committee, of which Rev. J. N. Murdock, D. D., was made chairman, recommended that "the directors of the Evangelical Baptist Benevolent and Missionary Society should have the right of a concurrent vote with the church in all the settlements of ministers to officiate in the stated services of the Tremont Temple."

The recommendation was accepted by both parties, and is now the rule.

Thus, from step to step, God led the church and Board to adopt a course which has secured harmony and a degree of prosperity such as were never before witnessed. At a glance, all discover the possibilities of a magnificent success. Money invested in this corporation pays great dividends for the cause of Christ. It aids in keeping open a large and attractive place in the heart of Boston, where the gospel is preached to an immense multitude, many of whom would not find a seat in any other place of worship, while it must ultimately provide a fund of several thousand dollars annually for missionary purposes.

Deacon Gilbert, as a member of the Board of Directors, watched over the interests of the Temple, with unfaltering zeal, to the close of life.

When others hesitated he held on in his course. To him, more than to any other man, we owe it that the Temple was not sold in the dark days succeeding 1860. Nor did he labor for himself, but to strengthen evangelical religion, and through it reach and move the world. When the Temple was called "a sponge, which absorbs easier than it exudes;" when a city pastor spoke of it as an element of denominational weakness; when the Board grew weary — though Mr. G. had been impoverished, like David faint yet pursuing and relying upon that Being whose interpositions had saved it in the past, he would exclaim, at the close of a tiresome debate, "Brethren, you may vote as you choose; the Temple will not be sold."

His heart was cheered by letters from various quarters, of which this, from the hand of Rev. D. C. Eddy, D. D., is a fair specimen: —

"I recognize the importance of the field of usefulness of the Temple. The right man could do more good there than anywhere upon the continent. It is a useful as well as a glorious place to labor. I believe a minister could live more for God, in one year at the Temple, than in a regular church edifice in ten."

The congregations were a source of perpetual enjoyment to him. The vast multitudes of young men were the subjects of his constant thought. Hundreds were spoken to by him who never forgot his words of cordial welcome. He did not rejoice in the prosperity of the Temple in any spirit of vain-glorying. He believed that if the Temple were emptied and its congregations were scattered, if the inspiring sights that have ever been witnessed when the gospel in its simplicity and with religious fervor has been proclaimed, should become a tale of by-gone days, the Baptist congregations in the city would see no sensible difference in their own. The congregation at the Temple is not drawn from others. Yet admit that other congregations do feel a slight draft upon them, Mr. Gilbert felt that the fact that the largest Protestant audience in America statedly listened to the truth as he understood it, was a matter for denominational congratulation and a cause for exultation, rather than an occasion for denunciation and jealous opposition.

CHAPTER XII.

PERSONAL RECOLLECTIONS.

DEACON GILBERT was a man to be remembered. He wore the appearance of a gentleman of the olden time. His bald forehead, white hair, black, glittering eyes, white neck-tie, and black dress gave him a clerical appearance, and made him a marked feature in any public assembly. He recognized his position, and understood the importance of allowing his influence to be felt. He consecrated his time, his talents, and his property to the service of Christ. He did not, like so many of our leading business men, act as though his time was too precious or his position too great to make it incumbent upon him to attend the social gatherings of the church, and exert his influence upon the young. He was a power in the church, because he lived in the church, and identified himself with its every interest. His house, his table, and his business were made subservient to the weal of the cause of Christ. Hence ministers and evangelists were sure of a welcome at his fireside. The young and inexperienced were sure of meeting sympathy, and of obtaining good counsel, in his counting-room.

It was Friday evening, March 6, 1863, when the writer came, a stranger, to No. 8 Beach Street. He had been invited to supply the desk on the coming

Sabbath, and feeling a desire to ascertain the condition of the church, by attending the prayer meeting, he had come on Friday.

Mr. Gilbert's greeting was cordial, his look was kind, but searching. The stranger had heard through previous pastors much of his idiosyncrasies of character, and was prepared to see in the lithe and slightly bent form of the builder of Tremont Temple a man distinguished for reserved power, and for a look that is accustomed to have its way. At once the measure was taken. It was not to Mr. Gilbert perfectly satisfactory. He was in doubt. He intimated that the church needed a pastor. As he was not in the presence of a candidate, the topic was changed. At tea the family evidenced that a strange face was not a strange sight. The habits of the deacon were seen to be peculiar. After tea the Bible was brought out. He read and prayed. That prayer revealed his heart. He longed for the prosperity of Zion, and asked God for a blessing to attend the coming of the preacher. We went to the house of prayer in company. The diary says, "Had a very good meeting — good spirit." Saturday was passed by the new comer among his friends. In the afternoon it began snowing, and by Sabbath morning every railroad was blocked, cars were taken off, and sleighs were brought into requisition. The sight affected and depressed the heart of the deacon. The minister smiled, and claimed that he liked a stormy day, as it revealed the grit and character of the soldiers of the cross. The Temple was nearly empty. None but the bravest were there. The paths were not broken. Those who did come literally pressed through difficulties to the house of God. They formed a part of that unconquered company who had withstood the trials, and overcome the difficulties, that at times threatened to undermine the foundations of their permanence and prosperity. The services did the church good. Their faces showed it. The prayer meeting in the evening, which the diary pronounced "exceedingly interesting," evidenced it. The letters that followed, inviting the preacher to become pastor, all referred back to that stormy day without, and to that glorious day within, the Tremont Temple.

At this time the question of sale was still agitating the minds of the denomination. A few facts will throw light upon the condition of affairs. The union that was a felt necessity on the part of all friends did not exist between the church and the Board. The church was under a cloud. They were poor, but they respected themselves. While they were willing to ask the co-operation of the Board, they were not willing to consent to the dictation of the Board. They claimed the right of choosing their pastor, and were only willing to refer his credentials to the Board. The church needed character. It needed strong men who were known and respected abroad, as well as men revered and respected at home. The individual who was repeatedly invited to become their pastor, claimed that laymen are called, as well as ministers, to walk the paths of trial and toil. In other words, it was felt that this church, while it throws open its doors to the poor and to the stranger, should contain within its membership and personal friends ability of brains and of pocket sufficient to sustain and manage the enterprise; that the principle embodied in the words of Christ, "Ye are the salt of the earth," ought not to be ignored; that there is a humanity in Christianity as well as a Christianity in humanity; that brain produces brain; that financial strength begets financial strength, just as spiritual power repeats itself in spiritual power. Feeling is well; but without reason it becomes a mountain torrent, turbulent and noisy. Talent is well; but unless it be consecrated to Christ, it will shed a brilliant light abroad, while it remains quite too cold at home. Money is well; but money cannot buy God's blessing, nor secure the salvation of a single soul. There must be a union of piety, of talent, and of financial strength. Poverty may figure well in the flowing numbers of the poet, but it amounts to but little in the cash accounts of the financier. It is not regarded as a blessing to be coveted, nor as a fact to be despised. The Tremont Temple could not be sustained as a poor-house, nor the pastor as a public pauper. This view of the condition of affairs met with a hearty response in the minds and hearts of some of the leading friends of the enterprise. Attempts were made to secure the services of the pastor alone. It was in vain. As a result, the Union and Tremont Street Baptist Churches came together, and formed a new organization, called the Union Temple Baptist Church. The dead past was buried. A bright future dawned upon the enterprise. Fresh life was infused into the Sabbath school, into the prayer meeting, and the congregation felt the influence. Days of fasting and prayer were held. The church looked to God for a blessing, and began at once to labor for the salvation of souls. At the outset it was difficult for Deacon Gilbert to get used to the new order of things. The thoughts of the church were turned into new channels. The church meeting, which had been a kind of a debating society, was done away with.

The prudential committee attended to matters of discipline, and introduced to the church those who were deemed worthy to be received. The executive committee took charge of the finances, and at once devised a system of raising money by subscription, which relieved the treasury, and provided for the wants of the society. To say that Deacon Gilbert at once heartily entered into the spirit of the new *régime* would be untrue. At first he felt called upon to take the direction of affairs into his own hands, as had been his custom. The pastor objected. There were three instances. Mr. G. minuted them in his diary. One Monday morning he proposed to talk the matter over. The pastor went with the deacon to his parlor. They spoke their minds. The new system was explained. From that time to the hour of the deacon's release, he was the kindest, the most considerate, of brothers. Henceforth there was no collision. The pastor respected and loved his deacon. The deacon respected and loved his pastor. They enjoyed each other's society in the house of God and elsewhere, and the pastor feels that he can adopt the language of the efficient secretary of the society, Solomon Parsons, Esq., who in a note says, "I bless God in permitting me in so humble a manner the honor of sharing the labors of the founder or originator of this great enterprise, and that I was able in some slight degree, after entering upon the duties of my office, to appreciate his labors and undertakings, and to aid him in his wishes and desires for the continuance and perpetuation of this noble work to those who shall come after him."

The Christian character of Deacon Gilbert rested upon immovable foundations, and shines forth in these public records. To learn his sacrifices, his toils, and devotion to the cause of Christ, the eye must become familiar with his private memoranda, and the ear with the unrecorded acts of a generous life. There is a vast pile of manuscript unreached. Here are letters to Charles Sumner, John P. Hale, and John Quincy Adams, to Abraham Lincoln and Andrew Johnson, showing that he felt the responsibilities of an American citizen and a Christian philanthropist. Again, topics such as "Consecration," "Devotion," "Humility," are treated at considerable length.

Here is another paper in which he enters into an argument to prove that the Temple was as strictly dedicated to the worship of Almighty God, notwithstanding it was let for secular purposes, as was any pewed church. This paper is without a date, but it is not difficult to understand why it was drawn up. Some one has been decrying the enterprise, because the large hall of the Temple is rented to, and used by those who obtain it, for secular purposes. The deacon, as is his wont, writes out his argument, and thenceforth wields it with force.

Another paper explains why it would be improper to place the deed of the Temple in the hands of the church. (It was the original design to do this when the debts were paid.) First, because the title from a church would not be valid, as a church is not recognized as a legal body; second, if a church were legal, moneyed institutions would not loan them money, as it would be injurious to their reputation to dispossess a church of a house in order to get their dues.

We have already seen that Mr. G. gave employment to men without distinction of color. The boy Thomas, to whom reference was made in the slave hunter's letter, is still in the city; and James Jones, who came to the North in the hold of a vessel, where he was packed away, having reached Boston, and being friendless and nearly famished, was brought to Timothy Gilbert, and remained in the employ of his friend until within a year of the death of the latter, and found pleasure in attending him night after night in his last sickness. These instances simply illustrate a life of rare devotion in ameliorating the woes of the friendless and the poor. The history of his friendship and friendly acts to the colored people is written in the book of God's remembrance, for it was the rule of his life not to let the right hand know what the left hand doeth. For forty years he occupied that elevated position to which God in his providence led the nation, where Abraham Lincoln died, — a position in the light of which the Declaration of Independence lost its glittering generalities, — where patriotism, love to God, and love to men made black men so white he could not see their blackness, and where narrowness and treason made white men so black he could not see their whiteness, — a position in which he recognized the manhood of American citizenship.

The following letter, the last ever written by his hand for the press, was printed in the "Watchman and Reflector" the week before he departed for the better land. It is the utterance of the friend of the slave, as he stood in the light of the eternal world.

Constitutional Rights.

The Declaration of Independence, which has always been recognized as the foundation of our constitutional government, asserts that all men are created free and equal, and are by their Creator entitled to life, liberty, and the pursuit of happiness.

The Constitution, Article I. Section 2, provides that representatives shall be apportioned among the several states according to the whole number of free persons, and three fifths of all other persons (Indians not taxed being the only exceptions).

If there are no slaves, then of course there are none to which the three-fifths rule can apply, but all are free persons. The only classes referred to in the Constitution are "free" and "all others;" no reference is made to color. The free people are the only people under the Constitution recognized as *the* people to form a government. The language of the Preamble is as follows:

"We, the people of the United States, in order to form a more perfect union, establish justice, insure domestic tranquillity, provide for the common defence, promote the general welfare, and secure the blessings of liberty to ourselves and our posterity, do ordain and establish this Constitution for the United States of America."

With the foregoing constitutional provisions, unless something can be proved to the contrary, can any part of the people of any state — and especially the truly loyal part—be excluded from participating in the government, under the Constitution, without violating its provisions?

By an act of Congress under the census of 1860, the number of representatives is fixed at 233, viz.—from the free states 149, and from the slave states 84—based upon a representative population of 29,806,801, three fifths only of the slave population being counted, which gives the ratio for each representative 126,845. But, counting the whole population, 31,209,742, as free, and dividing it by 233, the number of representatives fixed by the act of Congress, will give the ratio to each representative 133,947, which will give the former free states only 141, and the former slave states 92 representatives, and the same number of electors for president. By this it will be seen that the free states will lose eight, and the slave states gain eight representatives, making a change of sixteen votes in favor of the slave states, if the same people as before the rebellion are to be the sole electors, and to have the supreme power.

If the late slave population is excluded from the ballot in these states, and the freed people are placed at the mercy of their rebel masters whom they have *helped us* to subdue, does not every feeling of our heart cry out, in view of the indignities and barbarities they must suffer from those who have starved, tortured, and murdered our men while in their prisons and elsewhere?

The injustice, inequality, and unconstitutionality of this are further apparent from the fact that twenty-nine of these ninety-two representative and electoral votes (if this injustice is permitted) will be derived from counting said excluded class; otherwise they would be entitled to only sixty-three votes. This injustice and inequality are still further seen by comparing the population and the representative and electoral votes. The free-state population is two and twenty-eight one hundredths to one in slave states, excluding the slave population; but the representative and electoral votes will be only one and fifty-three one hundredths to one in slave states.

Thus, while we have been flattering ourselves that the rebels are conquered, does it not appear to be the reverse, if we surrender to them, not only *all* the political power they ever had, but reward them with this increase of power, without the *least* corresponding gain on our part? Will it not appear that they are the conquerors, and we the conquered? — they only losing, what to them was worse than useless, the right to hold property in slaves, which has always been an incubus upon the growth and prosperity of that section of the country, and gaining this increase of political power. If they secure from the free states only twenty-five additional votes, it would give them a majority in the House of Representatives; and is it unreasonable to suppose that number may be secured, and that an attempt may be made to repudiate some part or all of the debt created in bringing them into subjection?

How can we avoid these threatened evils, and the danger of another war, but by securing to all the people their constitutional right — the ballot?

A government like ours, even if we ignore the question of justice, formed to establish justice, and secure liberty, in order to be strong must be just to all its loyal subjects, securing to all equal rights and privileges. This is included in securing to each state a republican form of government. It was because slavery was unjust and oppressive that it was an element of weakness. It was the injustice of their claims, more than the physical or financial strength of the parties in the late civil war, that decided in favor of the victorious party.

If the question of equal rights to the freedman shall be the cause of another civil war in this country, who can doubt but that the God-fearing, sin-hating, and liberty-loving portion of our people, both North and South, *will*, by their prayers and efforts, give aid and comfort to those who are thus deprived of their just rights?

God, who is just, will defend the right, as in our late struggle; and *woe* to him that is found resisting his will.

T. G.

Boston, June, 1865.

Again he takes the pen, and gives utterance to his views concerning the right of suffrage for the black man, and publishes them in the "Christian Era": —

I have been exceedingly gratified and hopeful for the future of our country in the almost universal utterances I have seen in the press, and heard from the platform, in favor of the freedmen being admitted to all the rights of citizenship. Nothing short of this, I think, will secure to our government the favor of God, and through his favor and blessing the glorious future I see in store for this nation.

But in the restoration of the seceded states we are in danger of compromising with injustice and wrong. In the proclamation just issued by our president I think there is cause for alarm. He empowers William W. Holden, the newly-appointed provisional governor of North Carolina, as soon as it shall seem proper to call a convention of the loyal people of that state, to reorganize a state government, with an altered or amended constitution, in order that said state may be readmitted into the Union. He then prescribes that an elector, in order to be entitled to vote in calling said convention, must have the qualifications prescribed by the constitution and laws of that state previous to the passage of the (so called) ordinance of secession. This of course excludes all the freedmen. It further directs or provides that said convention so called, or the legislature that may thereafter assemble, shall, or may, prescribe the qualification of electors; which would be right if all the loyal people were represented in said convention; but they are not. This will leave the destiny and control of the state, for all future time, in the hands of the same class who have heretofore controlled its political status; only excluding those who *are proved* to have been in open rebellion, and such as refuse to take the prescribed oath of allegiance; *entirely excluding* the freedmen, who have been the only class in the seceded states during the rebellion that have been truly loyal. Such injustice cannot fail to provoke a just God, and call down his chastisements on the nation.

Under such circumstances, and with such a government so constituted, freedom can be but little more than a name. If the seceded states are to be restored, without any *other* guarantee for the security of the rights of the freedmen, then have the immense blood and treasure of the nation been expended without any adequate good being accomplished. But I cannot believe that God, who has been directing in all this terrible war, and, as I believe, has come down to deliver these oppressed ones, will permit the sword to be sheathed, and this nation restored to a lasting peace, until the freedmen are fully restored to all the rights of citizenship, and our nation shall stand forth with the motto taken from Holy Writ, and contained in our Declaration of Independence, inscribed upon all our laws and enactments, "God hath made of one blood all the nations of the earth."

I think this whole matter should be left open until the assembling of Congress at its next session, and that then they should be petitioned to pass uniform laws on the subject of naturalization for all the states, defining by a uniform rule who shall be entitled to vote, making no distinction on account of color. Petitions to this effect should be prepared and signed by every individual throughout the entire North, and also in the Southern States, so far as the inhabitants shall desire to do so, and forwarded to Congress at the opening of the session.

There is no provision in the Constitution that authorizes any distinction on account of color; and as the Constitution, Article IV. Section 4, makes it the duty of the United States to guarantee to every state a republican form of government, and to protect them against domestic violence, does not that provision make it the duty of the government to require of each state a republican constitution and laws?

A republic, according to Webster, is a state in which the exercise of the sovereign power is lodged in representatives elected by the people. Can they be said to be elected by the people if only half or two thirds of the loyal people are permitted to vote? Would Massachusetts be a republic, if all its laboring men were excluded from the elective franchise, or all its mechanics, or all not having a liberal education, or any other class or standard that had no reference to loyalty, moral character, or such degraded ignorance and imbecility as would disqualify them for exercising that trust? And if it would be anti-republican in Massachusetts, is it not anti-republican in North Carolina, or in South Carolina, or in Georgia, or in any other state?

While slavery existed, and the slaves were the goods and chattels of the people, they were not in any legal sense recognized as a part of the nation, only for the purpose of being counted to increase the number of representatives, and by it the legislative power of these states. But this was as unjust as it would be for the free states to count their oxen and horses to increase their representatives. But under that arrangement only three fifths were to be counted.

Now, as slavery is done away with, those who were slaves will of course be regarded as men; and henceforth not three fifths, but the whole, must be counted; thus increasing the representation in that proportion.

By the last census, the aggregate population of the ten states who seceded was four million seven hundred and forty-seven thousand five hundred and eighty-six free, and three million two hundred and forty-three thousand three hundred and thirty-two slave; but taking only three fifths of the slaves and adding to the free, makes their representative population six million six hundred and ninety-three thousand five hundred and eighty-four. Divided by one hundred and twenty-six thousand eight hundred and forty-five, the ratio of apportionment among the several states, taken in the aggregate, it will give those ten states fifty-two representatives; but on the fractional parts they were allowed one more, which make fifty-three representatives; then counting the whole number of freedmen, as will now be the case, instead of three fifths, they will be entitled to sixty-three representatives — a gain of ten; and this increased power is all to be intrusted to those who have been fighting us for four years, and have been doing all in their power to overthrow our government, with shot and shell, as well as by robbery and arson, by murdering and starving our men when in their hands, and by every species of barbarity that could be invented by devils incarnate. It is not the cause of the freedmen alone that I plead, but that of the millions who are to participate in the glory or degradation that this nation will reap, in the fruit that will follow their action, in the settlement of this matter. Mr. Sumner, in his eulogy on our late president, has shown Mr. Lincoln's views to have been in favor of the political equality of the races: let us pray that his mantle may fall upon his successor.

June 2. T. GILBERT

Here the warrior laid aside his pen. In May, 1866, Charles Sumner and Solomon P. Chase wrote as follows: —

SENATE CHAMBER, 1st May, 1866.

DEAR SIR: It will not be in my power to take any part at the approaching anniversary of the Anti-Slavery Society. My duty will keep me here.

I trust that the society which has done so much for human rights will persevere until these rights are established throughout the country on the impregnable foundation of the Declaration of Independence. This is not the time for any relaxation of the old energies. Slavery is abolished only in name. The slave oligarchy still lives, and insists upon ruling its former victims.

Believing, as I do, that the national government owes protection to the freedmen, so that they shall not suffer in their rights, I insist that it has plenary power over this great question, and that it may do anything needful to assure these rights. In this conviction I shall not hesitate at all times to invoke its intervention, whether to establish what are called civil rights or that pivotal right of all — the right to take part in the government which they support by taxation and by arms.

Accept my best wishes, and believe me, dear sir, faithfully yours,

CHARLES SUMNER.

THE PRESIDENT OF THE ANTI-SLAVERY SOCIETY.

Letter from Judge Chase.

WASHINGTON, May 1, 1866.

DEAR SIR: I cannot attend the annual meeting of the American Anti-Slavery Society, on the 8th, except by sincere wishes for the complete accomplishment of its purpose to achieve the deliverance of our country from the spirit as well as the fact of slavery.

Among the most urgent duties of the hour, I count that of pressing upon the intelligence and the conscience of our countrymen the expediency as well as the obligation of unqualified recognition of the manhood of man.

The nation has liberated four millions of the people from slavery, and has made them citizens of the republic.

That all freedmen are entitled to suffrage, on equal terms, is an axiom of free government. Neither color nor race can be allowed, without injustice and damage, as grounds of exception.

If, in the first movement towards national reconstruction, this truth had been distinctly recognized by an invitation to the whole loyal people of every state in rebellion to take part in the work of state reorganization, can it now be doubted that the practical relations of every state with the Union would have been already reëstablished, and with the happiest consequences?

Nothing is more profitable than justice. Does not suffrage promote security, content, self-respect, betterment of condition? With suffrage will there not be more productive labor than without? Will not suffrage insure order, education, respect for law, activity in business, and substantial progress?

I have heard the difference between the production of the lately insurgent states with universal suffrage, and the production of the same states without it, estimated at one hundred millions of dollars a year. At this rate, the injustice of the denial of suffrage will cost those states, will cost the nation, five hundred millions of dollars in five years — enough to pay nearly one fifth of the national debt.

Is it too much to expect that sensible and patriotic men in those states will, before long, see their true interest in their plain duty, and join hands with those who seek, not their injury or their humiliation, but their welfare and their honor, in equal rights for all?

However these things may be, this, at least, seems clear. The men who so long contended for justice to the enslaved, and now contend for justice to the emancipated, will not, cannot, must not cease their efforts till justice prevails.

Yours truly,

S. P. Chase.

Wendell Phillips, Esq.

Surely whoever reads these utterances will see that the foresight of the Christian was quite as clear as that of the statesmen who, for many a year, have stood upon the headlands of political distinction.

We have but little space left to describe Mr. G. as a friend, a father, and a brother in Christ. As a friend he was not demonstrative, but the needle was not truer to the pole than was he towards those he loved.

In reading his diary my own heart has been touched by his expressions of love. Well do I remember the grasp of the hand and the tear-dimmed eye as he would express his gratification in listening to some sermon.

In his friendship he was remarkably outspoken, but was more apt to blame than to praise. There are those who felt unkindly towards him because of his plain dealing. On one occasion I called his attention to the fact, and tried to show that no sensitive man would receive rebuke for mistakes unless words of good cheer were spoken when deserved. Well do I remember the effect produced. He wept, and when we bowed in prayer he lifted the gate, and allowed the current of love to flow forth unchecked until I felt swept on by its resistless force. Henceforth his life seemed changed in this regard, and praise was never lacking in his speech.

He was the friend of the servants of Christ. Evangelists found a home beneath his roof. He sympathized in their labors, and kept up a correspondence with them regarding their toils and victories.

It is not my province to enter obtrusively within the charmed circle of home. As a husband he was in his way a model. His house was his retreat. His wife and children were his companions.

He lived the life of a Christian in the midst of his family. The morning devotions, in which he was never hurried, and the evening chapter and prayer, will long be remembered by those who have heard his comprehensive and happily expressed petitions.

Said a friend, "He is slow in speech, but eloquent and fluent in prayer." He was ardently attached to the new version of the New Testament, and read it with untiring zest. It was his request that it should be honored when his funeral discourse was preached.

In his last sickness he manifested the characteristics which distinguished his life. He was full of invention, and never tired in constructing a bed or arranging a chair, so that he might find rest. There was no rest for the weary here. There was rest only in heaven.

Of him Rev. E. C. Mitchell writes in language glowing with a love that was the result of years of intimate intercourse. It is but just to say that had Deacon Gilbert been Mr. Mitchell's own father, he could not have watched over him more tenderly. His letter is dated Alton, Ill., where, as professor in the Theological Seminary, he has found a sphere of wide usefulness.

SHURTLEFF COLLEGE, October 18, 1865.

My first acquaintance with Deacon Gilbert was formed in the autumn of 1850, the first year of my course of study at Newton. I had been elected superintendent of the Milton Sabbath School in Blossom Street, and had been serving in that capacity for a month or two, coming into the city on Saturdays. Having learned that I was without any convenient stopping-place in the city, and sometimes spent the Sabbath at a hotel, Deacon Gilbert, with characteristic liberality, sent me an invitation to make his house my home during my connection with the school. There I found a truly Christian home. The first thing which impressed me was the atmosphere of consecration to Christ which pervaded the household. Everything he had was daily laid upon the altar of God.

Though doing an extensive business, and enjoying a large income, his domestic affairs were conducted upon the most economical scale. The diet at his table was always simple and plain; but to this any servant of Christ was welcome, and a great multitude of such guests have been entertained there. Missionaries, ministers, agents of benevolent organizations, fugitives from bondage, aged, infirm, or needy ones, of whatever class or condition, always found a kindly shelter and a free table at No. 8 Beach Street. His family and servants were so accustomed to this state of things that they were never surprised at the entrance of strangers, nor waited to consult him before making them welcome. That such unquestioning hospitality would sometimes be imposed upon by unworthy persons is to be expected; but he could not on that account forego the privilege of exercising his stewardship towards the Lord's poor. Whatever their motives or deserts, none could remain long under his roof without deriving positive benefit from the visit. Not only was his example and the whole conduct of his household instructive and impressive, but he had a quiet way of probing the views, and motives, and purposes of his visitors, and, if necessary, of earnestly inculcating the true principles of religion and humanity in their application to practical life. And then the family worship — morning and evening, never omitted or crowded out by the greatest pressure of business, always deliberate and prolonged as a service in which he loved to linger — was so emptying of self and so full of God, so manifestly near the throne and so tenderly warm with heartfelt affection for Jesus, that none could pass through it without some melting of soul and some quickening of holy impulses.

It was my privilege to be with him on one occasion which applied a pretty severe test to the strength of his faith. I refer to the time when the first Tremont Temple building was burned. This building was to him the embodiment of a great idea, the permanent establishment of a free gospel in the city, and a perpetually consecrated income for benevolent purposes. For nine years he had watched the financial progress of the enterprise, and found it to tally with his original calculations, and to give fair promise of speedily realizing his most sanguine hopes. Suddenly, on a certain Thursday evening, immediately after the Sabbath on which Mr. Colver preached his farewell sermon, and a few hours after an audience had retired from listening to the weekly lecture by my classmate, Charles R. Pattison, of Michigan, Deacon Gilbert was called from his bed to find the Temple in flames, and to see it, before daylight, converted into a mass of ruins. The family altar at 8 Beach Street, that morning, was a most interesting and instructive place. The cheerful submission to what for the moment seemed a completely dark and inexplicable event, accepting it as God's without being able to see God in it, and yet the assured and trustful perception by faith of God's wisdom, and grace, and faithfulness, manifested the true spirit of adoption. The day had hardly passed before the aspect of things was changed; the sun broke through the cloud, and he and all could see that God had greater things in store than even his far-reaching sagacity had conceived.

I shall ever regard it as a special favor of Providence that I was permitted to be with him in his last hours, and to witness the patience, humility, and faith, which formed so fitting a conclusion to a preëminently earnest Christian life. I have already furnished you with my notes of some of his last words, taken as they fell from his lips. There were many other words and incidents, not recorded, whose memory will dwell with me as an impulse towards the foot of the cross. Truly,

> "The chamber where the good man meets his fate
> Is privileged beyond the common walks of life,
> Quite on the verge of heaven."

It was an especially gratifying circumstance that he should have lived to see the virtual accomplishment of two prominent objects, to which the labors and prayers of his life were devoted more than to any others — the abolition of American slavery and the success of the Tremont Temple enterprise. He often alluded to this with thankfulness during his illness, and in speaking of the latter object never failed to couple with it expressions of affectionate confidence in the pastor whom God had made an instrument of its recent progress. I think you may congratulate yourself, my brother, and be grateful to God that you have sustained such a relationship to such a man. I trust that many of like faith and devotion to Christ may be raised up to assist you in the important duties devolving upon you.

Very truly yours in the gospel,

EDWARD C. MITCHELL.

We have spoken freely of what Deacon Gilbert did not understand. It may be well to state that none were misunderstood more than himself. That he was not appreciated, all will admit. When he died, a mighty moral force was withdrawn from the community, and what had been the central support of the Tremont Temple enterprise fell prostrate. He believed in the mission of the work there being performed. He saw that every blow there struck sent echoes into the future. Look into that recruiting room. Excited men listen. An excited man speaks. Men write down their names on paper. It is not much. The act was performed in a moment. Follow it. Those signatures made soldiers of men. They step forth from their homes and enter the camp. Multiply that one scene by thousands, and behold the result on the Rappahannock, on the James, in Georgia, among the mountains of Tennessee, wherever our soldiers swarm, and fight, and die, and you find, following that first act, the deafening roar of battle, the clash of arms, the crumbling of Confederacies, and the breaking up of rebellions.

That we can understand. Go to the prairies of the West, to the gold mines of California,—you cannot go beyond the reach of the influence of Tremont Temple, and so, necessarily, beyond the influence of this single man. It finds its lodgment in kindred breasts, and its embodiment in churches of like faith. A man with powers cultured and developed, whose boundless resources of love, and energy, and talent, and skill, are consecrated to the glory of Christ and the good of men, is a noble benefaction. His heart is the home and his body the servant of God. In his brain ideas take form, which, transplanted among men, grow up into institutions, laws, policies, and governments. The small men, of whom the race consists, could do little or nothing without the great men. The race would make no progress were it not that here and there, age after age, the inspiration of the Almighty, which giveth understanding, concentrates in some one man the intellectual force of multitudes of men. His free force, direct out of God's hand, is the lightning which kindles into a flame the dried fuel lying upon the heart-altars of men, and only waits an igniting spark to kindle into a flame which shall illumine the dark places of earth. Nations rise or fall in proportion as they have or lack men capable of building them up in intelligence, integrity, and justice, and of leading them forward to the accomplishment of magnificent purposes. Churches are liberal or the opposite, they are devoted or the opposite, they are social or the opposite, just in proportion as the gifts of manhood have been bestowed or withheld.

The Christian manhood of Deacon Gilbert was the outgrowth of the work of grace in his heart. As flowers take coloring from the earth in which their roots are imbedded, so was his Christian life tinged and colored by the qualities of his manhood, and by the influences which entered into the composition of his character. Christ builds on men as well as builds in men. Hence the faults and virtues of a man's character are chargeable to temperament, to nature, to the opportunities for culture, and the endowments of education possessed by him. Christianity has been likened to a seed planted in the heart. The strength of the root, and the height of the trunk, and the thrift of the tree, depend upon the soil. Rocky soil is bad — clear rock is worse. This fact saves Christianity from the shame and disgrace which have been stamped upon it by the sordidness, narrowness, and meanness of men. The tree was dwarfed and the fruit was poor because of the character of the soil in which it grew. Christianity changes the currents of man's nature as to direction, and it improves his quality. This fact makes manhood, which is broad, deep-cultured, strong, and brave, of priceless value. It exalts in our estimation the worth of education, of filling the mind with ennobling thought, and the heart with generous purposes. So soon as it accepts the rule of Heaven, and yields to Christ, its breadth, and depth, and strength give force and power to its new life. Had Timothy Gilbert never known Christ, his brain and heart-power, his industry and zeal, would have made him famed. Having known Christ, his goodness crowned his greatness, and made him the honored deacon, the generous Christian, and the noble man.

CHAPTER XIII.

MR. GILBERT'S DEATH. — NOTICES OF THE DECEASED. — HIS FUNERAL.

For twenty years Deacon Gilbert had been a great sufferer from a chronic disease of the heart. He endured far more than any one knew. The *post-mortem* examination revealed ossification of one of his lungs, dropsy in the chest and in the heart, and a general decay of the forces of life. He had talked little about his distressed periods, but tried to live so that his grave should be to him as welcome as his bed. All remember his deathly-pale face, his difficulty in breathing, the look of agony that flitted across his features, and the cheery speech that broke from his lips. He described his pain to be like the incision of a knife; yet he never complained, and seemed to make it his aim so to live that at all times he could adopt the language of Christ — "Not my will, but thine, O God, be done."

He was with us the last time on the 25th of June, 1865. It was Sabbath morning. The sermon, he was pleased to say, comforted his heart. The text, "Let love be without dissimulation," suggested a train of thought which his whole life had illustrated.

His disease — dropsy of the chest — caused him intense suffering, and made him very anxious for his release. He had the care of Dr. William Wesselhoeft, a most skilful physician; but from the first there was no hope of recovery.

On Sabbath, July 9, his feet began to swell, and symptoms of dissolution appeared. When his attention was called to them, he remarked, "There cannot be so good news as that I am dying." Then, in a moment, he added, "I don't know how long I shall suffer, but I hope I shall not be left to complain. At times I fear that I desire to escape suffering more than to glorify Jesus."

On another occasion he said, "It is not much matter about me; let the rest of you apply yourselves to the duties of life. You cannot save sinners, but you can let your light shine. They cannot resist the power of that light."

Then his thoughts came back to the Temple: "So far as I have had any thing to do with keeping that place open, it was for the glory of Christ. Don't let any one call it mine. Let them call it Christ's." Then he prayed, "O Jesus, if it be thy will, dispose the hearts of liberal men to free Tremont Temple from debt, so that it may become a lasting blessing to the destitute and the lost. The young members do not know much about what it has cost to rescue it from failure. Ask the pastor to urge upon the young men to prepare to meet their God. This is a very common expression, but in the light of eternity it has terrible meaning."

Duties had called the pastor away. He did not expect to see his beloved deacon again in the flesh. But being telegraphed, upon learning his condition he hastened home. After the reply came, stating that the pastor would be home on Wednesday evening, he asked to live. At six the pastor came. He found his senior deacon very feeble, and almost in a dying state. It was a joyous greeting. The old smile was on his face. The flash was in his eye. The kiss of welcome was given, and after the prayer was offered, taking the pastor's hand in his, he said, "Now, Lord, lettest thou thy servant depart in peace." But a week of agony remained.

Patiently and meekly he bore his yoke until the following Sabbath. He longed to die on Saturday night. He was disappointed. They thought him dying, but he lived. Sabbath morning found him sitting up in his large chair by the east window, with a seat beside him, waiting for his pastor. Upon his arrival the deacon greeted him with delight, and asked to be brought *en rapport* with the sermon and the line of thought. The uses of affliction were the theme. He listened to the statement of the doctrine, and the lesson drawn therefrom, joined in the prayer that followed, and was content. In the afternoon he felt that his wife and child held him back from God; and so he asked them to kneel by his bedside, "to let go of him," and "pray for his release." The same request was made of others. Monday his sufferings were intense, yet he was sublimely patient. Tuesday the doctor prescribed opium. He waited until his pastor came and prayed; heard him with an unclouded brain, then took the opiate, and, in an unconscious state, lingered on until Wednesday morning, when his uncaged spirit winged its way homeward to God.

The scenes of that sick chamber deserve photographing. They show how grandly a Christian may enter upon the last conflict, and go forth wreathed in victory.

On one occasion, in the midst of intense suffering, he found great comfort in these lines, which seemed to give expression to his thought: —

THE AGED BELIEVER AT THE GATE.

I'm kneeling at the threshold, weary, faint, and sore,
Waiting for the dawning, for the opening of the door,
Waiting till the Master shall bid me rise and come
To the glory of his presence, to the gladness of his home.

A weary path I've travelled, 'mid darkness, storm, and strife,
Bearing many a burden, struggling for my life;
But now the morn is breaking; my toil will soon be o'er;
I'm kneeling at the threshold; my hand is on the door.

Methinks I hear the voices of the blessed as they stand,
Singing in the sunshine of the sinless land;
O, would that I were with them, amid their shining throng,
Mingling in their worship, joining in their song!

The friends that started with me have entered long ago;
One by one they left me struggling with the foe.
Their pilgrimage was shorter, their triumph sooner won;
How lovingly they'll hail me when my toil is done!

With them the blessed angels, that know nor grief nor sin;
I see them by the portals, prepared to let me in.
O Lord, I wait thy pleasure; thy time and way are best;
But I'm wasted, worn, and weary — O Father, bid me rest!

And so he passed from the toils of earth to the rest of heaven — his life-work done, and well done. He was fitted of God to bear the yoke placed upon him. A different kind of man would have given his best thoughts to his business. He gave them to God.

Through evil as well as through good report, Timothy Gilbert adhered to his purpose to establish in the heart of the city of Boston a "free place of public worship." That work accomplished after the toil of a quarter of a century, he died content.

The city has lost a benefactor, a patriot, and a statesman. His eye pierced the vistas of the future; his earnest words warned of danger; his purse opened to every call for aid, and his pen was wielded in defence of those principles, which, after years of strife, have become prized above rubies, and promise to redeem a continent from the thraldom of slavery.

Upon whom shall his mantle fall? His history has little of romance, and less of feats that excite wonder. It is distinguished by the steady tramp of the true soldier, who, from the hour of his enlistment to the hour of his release, kept step to the music of love, led by the Captain of our salvation, who on earth made it his meat and his drink to do the will of our Father who is in heaven.

That he was missed, we have only to turn to the notices of the press, and the resolutions of different societies in which he had held a conspicuous place, to find abundant evidence.

The Board of the Evangelical Baptist Benevolent and Missionary Society at once took action, and proposed to bury him at the expense of the corporation, which had been largely fostered by his hand. The resolutions offered and passed embodied the leading traits of his character, and are as follow: —

At a meeting of the Board of Directors of the Evangelical Baptist Benevolent and Missionary Society, convened at Social Hall, Tremont Temple, July 20, 1865, the following resolutions were adopted in reference to the death of the late Deacon TIMOTHY GILBERT.

Whereas, God, in his all-wise providence, has called our late associate, Deacon Timothy Gilbert, from the activities of earth to the enjoyments of heaven, it seems proper that this Board should place on record some suitable memorial of his character and worth.

Deacon Gilbert has been honorably identified, for more than forty years, with the interests of the Baptist denomination in this city. During this long period he has been actively identified with the leading public enterprises for the advancement of the cause of Christ. He was one of the few Christian men who laid the foundations of Newton Theological Institution in sacrifice and prayer. He was also an early patron of the cause of missions to the heathen, and many of our missionaries, both among the living and the dead, have shared his benefactions and hospitalities. He was emphatically a lover of good men, and engaged in all good works.

It was while engaged in efforts for the religious instruction of the adult youth and strangers thronging the city, that he conceived the idea of establishing the Tremont Temple enterprise as a free place of worship. His labors and sacrifices in connection with this enterprise are so well known that no detailed account of them in this connection is necessary. His unwearied efforts, his steady courage, and his large pecuniary offerings in this behalf, entitle him to the gratitude of the friends of Christ, and the success of his work there constitutes his best and most enduring monument. His labors are ended, and he has entered into his rest. Impressed with a sense of our great personal loss in the removal of our venerable friend and brother from our earthly counsel, we hereby tender to his afflicted family our sincere condolence in this hour of their deep domestic sorrow.

J. W. Converse,	Cyrus Carpenter,
J. W. Merrill,	Frederick Gould,
G. W. Chipman,	Solomon Parsons, Secretary,
G. C. Goodwin,	Joseph Sawyer,
J. H. Converse,	Chas. S. Kendall,
Joseph Story,	G. W. Little,
L. B. Marsh,	Jesse Tirrell.

His funeral was attended in the Temple by a large concourse of citizens, conspicuous among whom were the piano-forte manufacturers, who assembled in a body, and escorted his remains beyond the city limits. The clergy of the Baptist denomination were present, with the exception of his former pastor and much beloved friend, Rev. Rollin H. Neale, D. D., who was absent from the city. The prayers of Drs. Stow and Eddy in the Temple were brim full of appreciative sympathy, and breathed a spirit of thankfulness to God for the gift of such a life to the church and to the world.

Dr. Hague, for many years his friend, spoke as follows: —

"The cause of Christ and truth, of freedom and humanity, suffers a loss by the death of Timothy Gilbert, a man of sterling excellence, a true Christian philanthropist. The Temple is his monument. Every stone and rafter are vocal with his memory. To buy Tremont Theatre and convert it into a church edifice for the free preaching of the gospel, as he did, a quarter of a century ago, was one of the bravest acts which signalize the history of Christian benevolence in Boston. His whole life-course, for half a century, was in keeping with that movement. He regarded the measure as a want of the times, and he staked his fortune upon its success. He made money in order to USE it for his Master. Amid the agitations of the country, in the fluctuations of business, he has lost much, no doubt; but he has saved much, which is well invested in an enterprise, the fruits of which are 'heavenly treasures,' to be garnered year by year. He lived and died the friend of the oppressed, the champion of the right. It was a memorable day, when, in the heat of the contest about the fugitive slave law, he advertised in the public journals that any needy fugitive might find a home at his house, No. 8 Beach Street! Theodore Parker made a call there forthwith, to see the man and the place, and to express his surprise that there was such a house in Boston. The act was heroic; but it was like him. Brave old soldier of the cross! He has fought a good fight, he has *kept the faith*, and has gone to receive the crown of righteousness which the Lord will give to all that love him, and the least of the little ones that believe in him, faithful even unto death."

Rev. Nathaniel Colver, D. D., had been expected, but was delayed by the train; and so the pastor followed in a brief delineation of the deacon's character, and reserved for the following Sabbath a more complete view of that finished life. In the coffin lying beneath the high roof of the Temple, Timothy Gilbert looked the man. A smile lingered upon his features, and the glory of a Christian's hope seemed to shed the halo of its light upon that scene of death. Turning from the coffin to the crowd, the pastor said, —

" The inquiry presses itself upon my heart as I turn from the contemplation of this heroic life — Is there no young man here, who, influenced by a similar purpose to glorify God, shall take the place left vacant by a Cobb, a Safford, and a Gilbert, and whose life of devotion to the interests of Christ's cause shall result in the planting of churches, in strengthening the hands of the ministry, in aiding forward revivals, in pushing on the car of salvation to the rescue of thousands from a life of shame here, and a life of misery hereafter?

" If so, welcome to such a field as their feet never trod, to such visions as their eyes never beheld. The world waits in its agony for the aggressive march of aggressive Christians.

'Will ye play, then, will ye dally
With your music and your wine?
Up! it is Jehovah's rally;
God's own arm hath need of thine.

'On! let all the soul within you,
For the truth's sake, go abroad;
Strike! let every nerve and sinew
Tell for ages — tell for God.' "

At his burial a most impressive scene was witnessed. The concourse of citizens and friends was large. Deacon Gilbert was buried beside his first wife in Mount Auburn, in a tomb which he had prepared. The sun was setting as we stood beside the open grave. We sung his favorite hymn, "Rock of ages, cleft for me," and then laid aside the sacred dust. The prayer, offered by Rev. O. T. Walker, will never be forgotten. It brought tears to every eye as it portrayed our loss, and thrilled every heart with joy as it described the Christian's gain. We saw him at rest with Jesus, beneath the shadow of the throne, surrounded by the early loved, and close to the heart of his loving Master, who had loved him first and loved him last, on whose strong arm the beloved disciple had leaned in his weakness, and in whose strength and grace he rested his every hope. As we turned from the sleeping form, and listened to the falling earth, which told us that his decaying remains were being committed to their kindred element, — earth to earth, dust to dust, — we thought of the general resurrection, through our Lord Jesus Christ, at whose coming, to judge the world, the earth and sea shall give up their dead; when the corruptible bodies of those who sleep in him shall be made like unto his glorious body, according to the mighty working whereby he is able to subdue all things unto himself. And as we looked upon the bent form of a mourning wife, and the tear-dimmed eyes of weeping friends, we derived comfort from those words of Hiller, which found their way to our hearts and gave expression to our thoughts as we went homeward: —

"We wait for thee, all-glorious One!
We look for thine appearing;

We hear thy name, and on the throne
We see thy presence cheering.
Faith even now
Uplifts its brow,
And sees the Lord descending,
And with him bliss unending.

"We wait for thee, through days forlorn,
In patient self-denial;
We know that thou our guilt hast borne
Upon the cross of trial.
And well may we
Submit with thee
To bear the cross and love it,
Until thy hand remove it.

"We wait for thee with certain hope;
The time will soon be over;
With child-like longing we look up,
Thy glory to discover.
O, bliss to share
Thy triumph there,
When home with joy and singing,
The Lord his saints is bringing!"

www.ingramcontent.com/pod-product-compliance
Lightning Source LLC
LaVergne TN
LVHW010250110826
845151LV00004B/1434
9781425522995